Pamela Burton Landscapes

PAMELA BURTON LANDSCAPES

Foreword by Robert A. M. Stern

Princeton Architectural Press
New York

Published by
Princeton Architectural Press
37 East 7th Street
New York, NY 10003

For a free catalog of books, call 1 800 722 6657
Visit our website at www.papress.com

Acquisitions Editor: Clare Jacobson
Project Editor: Laurie Manfra
Designer: Paul Wagner

Special Thanks to: Nettie Aljian, Sara Bader,
Nicola Bednarek, Janet Behning, Becca Casbon,
Carina Cha, Tom Cho, Penny (Yuen Pik) Chu,
Carolyn Deuschle, Russell Fernandez,
Pete Fitzpatrick, Jan Haux, Linda Lee, John Myers,
Katharine Myers, Steve Royal, Dan Simon,
Andrew Stepanian, Jennifer Thompson, Joe Weston,
and Deb Wood of Princeton Architectural Press
—Kevin C. Lippert, publisher

Library of Congress
Cataloging-In-Publication Data
Burton, Pamela.
Pamela Burton landscapes. — 1st ed.
    p.   cm.
ISBN 978-1-56898-965-5 (alk. paper)
1. Burton, Pamela. 2. Landscape architecture—
United States. I. Title.
SB470.B88B87 2010
712.092—dc22
                          2010009120

Contents

Foreword / Robert A. M. Stern

Amidst the torrent of discourse about landscape—discourse that, though important, often seems far removed from the natural world—Pamela Burton's monograph, like her work, is nothing short of reassuring, celebrating the age-old complementary relationships between building design, garden design, and horticulture. To look at her work is to enter a beautiful world of colors and textures, varied surfaces and vistas. Burton's gardens bring to contemporary architecture that extra dimension of specificity—a sense of place and time. As one reads the descriptions of her gardens, and even more so experiences them in person, one forgets the virtual reality that preoccupies too many in her profession and remembers how inventively the art of landscape architecture can bless our increasingly complex built environment with the hand of Mother Nature.

Unlike most of her peers, Pamela deploys her talent and extraordinary vision both to the design of grounds for private residences and to public places. I have had the good fortune to work with her on one project of each type, and have seen firsthand how she gives the same seriousness of purpose and liveliness of art to each. At The Century, a condominium tower in Los Angeles that offers residents the privacy of an estate without the burden of upkeep, Pamela's gardens—expansive lawns, mature trees, and drought-tolerant plantings organized around a reflecting pool—create a variety of spaces, from informal rooms with outdoor fireplaces for entertaining to intimate arbor-covered seating areas. A similar diversity of places, from quiet to active, enriches the Calabasas Civic Center, where she took inspiration from the arid hills above the sloping site, animating the space between the public library and city hall with a grove of olive trees, a plaza, and an amphitheater that complement the Mediterranean architecture of the buildings.

At the core of Pamela's work is an understanding of the intersection of nature and artifice, and the message that the organization of our homes, towns, and cities complements and to an extent replicates the structure of our natural world. In accommodating the range of needs that each project imposes, she never loses sight of beauty. Her art is knowing how to create places that serve the human spirit.

1. Tile Pool, Elyn Zimmerman, digital print,
Malibu Beach House, 2005

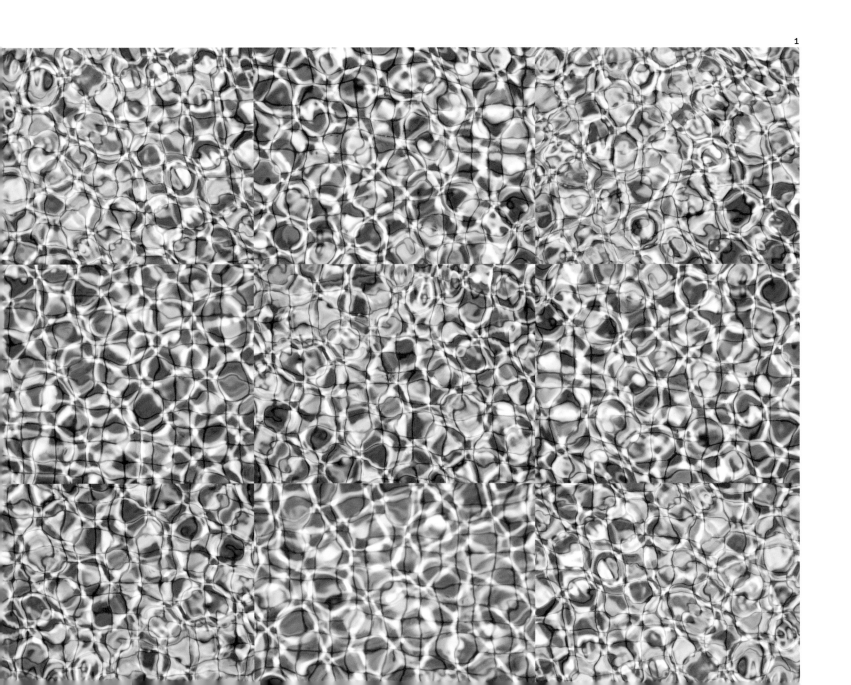

Introduction

Having lived in Los Angeles for most of my adult life, I have been instilled with a tremendous respect for the workings of its natural forces. To begin to understand where you live and how to cultivate your surroundings, it is important to internalize these forces of nature—the cycles of earth, air, fire, and water. This means scrutinizing the topographical features and giving great thought to what you can give to the Earth and what it can give back to you.

A garden or landscape has to have a big idea, otherwise the result might be mere arbitrary groups of plantings. A big idea—one that is simple, harmonious, and perceptible—is the product of a totality of experience. While the dialectic of working with clients has always been a source of creative growth and challenge for me, it has been through my encounters with my own gardens that I have been able, by necessity or desire, to fearlessly explore the world of ideas. In these spaces, I have been free to make radical cuts or simply take my time exploring.

It was during my undergraduate years at the University of California, Los Angeles (UCLA) studying art, design, and ornamental horticulture that I discovered that what I wanted most was to create landscapes. I felt that the best way to approach this vocation was through architecture, because these fields are so intimately connected. Visiting architects such as Charles Gwathmey, César Pelli, and Yoshio Taniguchi, and faculty members Craig Hodgetts, Eugene Kupper, and Tim Vreeland, each in their own way, encouraged students to think about the big picture. It was then that I came to understand that landscape architecture is not simply about gardening; it's about building a hierarchy of spaces that can be viewed as having cultural context and meaning.

Of the UCLA faculty, Charles Moore and Bill Mitchell were the most interested in landscape design. In their 1988 book *The Poetics of Gardens*, they emphasized that to make a garden is, first of all, to shape a space:

An object, which can be a building, tree, bush or birdbath, can stand alone in space, visible from all sides, or it can merge into the boundary of the space....The space between...is for the designer...a palpable something, which can be shaped precisely by walls and floors and ceilings or can erode and fade away, around a corner and out of sight, in picturesque ambiguity.[1]

Moore and Mitchell described the art of the garden designer as being similar to that of the architect:

> The ground plane is the natural starting point, and vertical elements can be raised from it to bound and focus spaces. Roofs and canopies can be added where shelter is needed. Connections can be made by forming openings, and sequences of movement through the spaces can be composed.[2]

Gradually I came to understand that the fundamental difference between designing a building and designing a garden is that a building's floors are planes (generally horizontal, occasionally slightly tilted), while the earthen floor of a garden site is seldom as organized or neatly cornered. Landscapes invite and insist upon a certain wildness. In them, walls and hedges form both horizontal and vertical elements, while the sky and tree canopy act as a kind of architectural ceiling.

At this time, I also worked at Ace Gallery and participated in the installations of earth-work artists, including Robert Smithson and Michael Heizer. Helping to construct Sol LeWitt's ephemeral wall drawings, I was inspired by the way colors overlapped. Likewise, Robert Irwin's scrim pieces and Elyn Zimmerman's observations of nature through photography, graphite drawings, and stone and water environments informed me about working with light, space, and perception.

When designing gardens, I think of myself as shaping distinctive outdoor rooms in the process of forming spatial axes and proportions of height and width, then creating exploratory paths that serve as connections between those garden rooms. In addition, elements such as openings, lighting, temperature (shade and water), sounds, and furnishings must be considered. I begin with a topographical survey and examine issues of grading, drainage, and underground utilities. I evaluate what trees exist and what kinds might be introduced. I study the site's horizontal and vertical measurements in order to incorporate existing foliage and the peculiarities of terrain. I love thinking about spatial organization, how people move through a place, how a series of spaces is connected, and how objects and materials frame and form the proportions. As Moore observed, one of the garden designer's first tasks is to consider the lay of the land and to decide how to modify its surface to receive construction, water, and plants.

My growing awareness of architecture and landscape as complementary forms of the same process was confirmed, when, at twenty-two years old, I took time off from studying at UCLA to visit Japan. There, in the gardens and temples, I observed the power of aesthetic simplicity and experienced the way in which the fusion of nature and architecture connected

2

3

4

me to something infinite and deep. I recognized these qualities as aspects of how I wanted to approach my work.

During this time, certain philosophies crystallized my ideas about the relationship of Japanese architecture and landscape to the development of modernism in architecture and landscape design. In the 1930s, German modernist architect Bruno Taut moved to Japan and visited Katsura Detached Palace. He was amazed to realize that for three hundred years, Japanese designers had already been applying many of the principles of modernism to their work. In his 1937 book *Fundamentals of Japanese Architecture*, Taut wrote that, like Japanese architects, what modernist architects sought was "an idealized conception of cleanliness, clarity, simplicity, cheerfulness, and faithfulness to the materials of nature."[3] The Katsura Detached Palace exemplified modernist ideas, such as the integration of nature and architecture, sliding planes, and framing of views. Their stroll gardens were comprised of cinematic sequences of spatial relationships between pavilions, paths, water elements, and viewing platforms. Moore understood it as a collection of garden rooms and rocks, flowers, bowers, and teahouses choreographed into a pilgrimage route. It is not only a collection in space, but an ordering in time.

Later, Leonard Koren, a fellow student at UCLA, wrote a book on *wabi-sabi*, the design philosophy that underlies a great deal of traditional Japanese art and architecture. Koren showed the similarities and differences between the ideals of modernism and the principles of wabi-sabi.[4] Both philosophies sought to avoid any decoration not integral to an object, structure, or arrangement, and each was a radical departure from earlier traditions. But while

2. Tofuku-ji Temple Garden, Kyoto
3. Saiho-ji Temple Garden, Kyoto
4. Detail of threshold, Ryoan-ji Temple, Kyoto

modernism can be described as seamless, polished, and smooth, wabi-sabi can be described as earthy, imperfect, and variegated. Modernism expressed faith in progress, was future oriented, and believed in the control of nature. The philosophy of wabi-sabi does not believe in progress, it is present oriented, and it believes in the fundamental uncontrollability of nature. In my practice, I seek to work from the threshold where these two philosophies meet. To me it is a place of energy, occasional opposition, and potential elegance.

On American shores, architects Irving Gill and Frank Lloyd Wright worked early in their careers for Louis Sullivan, who, during the later 1800s in Chicago, was a pioneer of modernist design. In 1892 Sullivan wrote in *Engineering Magazine*, "We should refrain entirely from the use of ornament in order that our thought might concentrate acutely upon the production of buildings well formed and comely in the nude."[5] Affirming this idea in his 1913 essay "Ornament and Crime," Adolf Loos wrote "cultural evolution is synonymous with the removal of ornament from articles in daily use."[6] Midcentury garden design revolved at first around the ideas and work of architects like Richard Neutra and Rudolph Schindler. They had absorbed Wright's emphasis on simplicity in design and materials and the fusion of inside and outside—a philosophy that Wright honed during his travels to Japan. During this time, Los Angeles-based modernists created "the pavilion in the garden"—houses that grew up from their sites and embraced them.

The ideals of modernist landscape design were not set forth in California alone. In the late 1930s, three student renegades started a commotion at Harvard's Graduate School of Design in Cambridge, Massachusetts. In the footsteps of Thomas Church and Edward Huntsman-Trout, who were already working in California, Dan Kiley, Garrett Eckbo, and James Rose turned away from designing gardens for viewing. Instead they focused on designing outdoor spaces for living, incorporating terraces and pools around which families could relax, entertain, and renew their relationship with nature. These spaces were meant to be affordable, easy to maintain, and accessible from the house. In turn, this approach gave rise to outdoor furnishings designed to be part of a seamless environment that blurred the distinction between inside and out. Outdoor rooms, the use of plate glass, sliding doors, and borrowed landscapes and the use of multiple viewpoints or perspectives all enlarged the amount of usable area and enhanced the feeling of open space.

To demonstrate how modernist ideas were embedded in the midcentury gardens and houses of A. Quincy Jones, Joseph van der Kar, John Lautner, Neutra, Schindler, and many more, I wrote, with Marie Botnick and Kathryn Smith, the book *Private Landscapes: Modernist Gardens in Southern California* (2002). In her essay, Smith wrote:

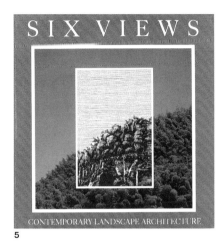

5

6

There is a strong and independent tradition in Southern California that can be traced back to as early as 1911 in the work of Irving Gill.…By the time the post–World War II building boom was over, Southern California could boast the largest concentration of modern houses in the world.…These architects all shared a common approach that combined modern forms with a distinct understanding and sympathy for the natural site and its particular characteristics of terrain and vistas. It was this approach more than anything else that distinguished these architects from their European contemporaries.[7]

By the 1980s various landscape architects were exploring threshold spaces: George Hargreaves, between landscape and graphic design; Martha Schwartz, between landscape and art installations; and Peter Walker, between landscape and formal sculpture gardens. I, in turn, gravitated toward those affinities between the tradition of California modernists Neutra and Schindler, with their focus on the integration of landscape and architecture, and Japanese concepts of gardens as both place of refuge and journey. In 1986, with Dextra Frankel, I cocurated the exhibition Six Views: Contemporary Landscape Architecture, which explored these shifting, innovative approaches.

My perspective on the relationship between modern landscape architecture and modern art has continued to develop and expand through the example of many artist friends. Astrid Preston taught me how landscapes may be viewed as symbolic creations—for example, symbolic layers of consciousness. Preston's paintings demonstrate the power of shadows and explore the mysterious meaning of absence.

5. Exhibition catalog, 1986
6. *Near Paradise*, Astrid Preston, oil on canvas, 1986

7

8

9

10

7. Lita Albuquerque constructing
Blue Triangle for Rocca Way House, blue
pigment and earth, 1978
8. *Agave Plant: R,O,Y,W,G,B,V,* John
Baldessari, 1999-2008
9. The hills of Malibu, California
10. View of the valley of Ojai, California

In a garden the creation of shadows can be just as important as the vegetation—a point that Jun'ichiro Tanizaki made when writing *In Praise of Shadows*.[8] From Preston I learned to appreciate ambiguity and to savor the experience of being uncertain where the sky stops and the earth begins. Being comfortable with ambiguity, one can be comfortable with not knowing, with letting events and situations take on a life of their own, apart from our desires to control them. I wanted the paths and gardens I designed to be important for the journeys they invite us to undertake, not only (or especially) for bringing us somewhere else.

From Lita Albuquerque I learned that in order to make a powerful and sustaining image or statement, "less" can truly be "more." In her early work she applied raw pigment directly to the earth. The colors and forms had a very strong impact, highlighting everything that was nearby. Artist John Baldessari taught me that humor and a lighthearted touch can be attractive and are powerful ways to bring complexity into a project. Baldessari's work exemplifies the power of recontextualizing ideas and imagery—for example, by using traditional materials, metaphors, and technologies in nontraditional and innovative ways.

Throughout my career I have been very influenced and informed by where I lived—the hills of Malibu and the valley of Ojai. I have learned repeatedly that the success and value of spaces are not always seen immediately; they are felt. Many defining edges and threshold meetings can go into making a space resonant: proportions of inside and outside, light and shadow, nature and cultivation, social needs and solitude. My own living spaces became places to experiment and explore by instinct; if I fell, I didn't hurt myself. I replanted.

As a result of disparate life experiences, certain characteristics in my design evolved. Garden and landscape became one grand idea—an integrated whole. Under an apparent spilling of vegetation was a rigorously quiet structure, within which the Japanese principles of wabi-sabi occur. These include spontaneity, randomness, and the unexpected. In addition to this interplay between structure and randomness, I learned to create contrasts between inside and outside, between the controlled and the uncontrollable. I emphasized a sophisticated, elegant, subtle use of plant materials, often with strong visual impact. Influenced by our family citrus ranch in Ojai, California, I have made extensive use of retaining walls of native stone, both as a visual element and to create overlays of usable space. Often these walls are linked together to create enclosures. It is important to create spaces that provide refuge for contemplation and beauty. I also like to employ metaphorical and symbolic elements nourished by my readings of mythology, history, and poetry.

From reading *The Experience of Place* by writer Tony Hiss, I learned that we have built into us two different systems for organizing our perceptions—the narrowing focus of ordinary consciousness, and the more inclusive approach of simultaneous perception. I always like to promote, as Hiss writes, "a rich variety of experiences in a place to stay connected with our environment and with other people."[9]

Over the years, I've found the most important thing is to maintain a balance between four arenas of the creative life: looking, thinking, drawing, and making. Looking is about feeding the creative soul, about receiving images from travel, art, and daily life. Thinking is about analyzing and making conceptual connections, putting one's work and experiences within different theoretical frameworks. Drawing is about recording insights, taking imaginative leaps, and bringing ideas and images of oneself and putting them onto paper. Building is about manifesting those images and ideas, implementing them while editing, refining, and revising. I take great pleasure in each of these interconnected components of the creative process.

In the end, a garden takes on its own layers of time and meaning, and I do not have to spell them out completely. I have come to be satisfied if it appears as if I didn't do anything. Arriving at that point has taken a tremendous amount of work; it is the constant process of editing that lets a garden age and endure, deepening and leaning into its own story.

This book is organized by chapters that bring together clusters of private and public projects in order to show the interrelationships and crossovers between them. I do not consider my private and public projects as different bodies of work; they inform one another. My emphasis in landscape is on creating gardens that inspire a sense of personal well-being, beauty, and physical and metaphorical resonance of aesthetics and proportion. Although my ideas have been fed and informed by my own threshold experiences, internal and external, ultimately, landscape architecture is about making people feel comfortable in spaces, among their family, friends, and with themselves. My goal is to create gardens that are experienced and thoroughly enjoyed as more than the sum of their individual parts.

NOTES

1   Charles W. Moore, William J. Mitchell,
    and William Turnbull, Jr., *The Poetics of Gardens*
    (Cambridge, MA: The MIT Press, 1988), 26.

2   Ibid.

3   Bruno Taut, *Fundamentals of Japanese
    Architecture*, 2nd ed., (Tokyo: The Society
    for International Cultural Relations, 1937), 9;
    quoted in Sandra Kaji-O'Grady, "Authentic
    Japanese Architecture after Bruno Taut:
    The Problem of Eclecticism," *Fabrications* 11, no.
    2 (2001): 4.

4   Leonard Koren, *Wabi-Sabi for Artists, Designers,
    Poets & Philosophers* (Berkeley, CA: Stone
    Bridge Press, 1994), 25–29.

5   Thomas S. Hines, *Irving Gill and the Architecture
    of Reform*: *A Study in Modernist Architectural
    Culture* (New York: The Monacelli Press,
    2000), 129.

6   Ibid.

7   Pamela Burton and Marie Botnick, *Private
    Landscapes: Modernist Gardens in Southern
    California* (New York: Princeton Architectural
    Press, 2002), 7.

8   Jun'ichiro Tanizaki, *In Praise of Shadows*, trans.
    Thomas J. Harper and Edward G. Seidensticker
    (New Haven, CT: Leete's Island Books, 1977),
    29–30.

9   Tony Hiss, *The Experience of Place* (New York:
    Vintage Books, Random House, Inc., 1990), 99.

I. INFLUENCES & STRATEGIES

1

Projects in the late 1970s allowed me to explore several important themes: the joining of formal planning with spontaneous exuberance, the contrast of Southern California's wild chaparral landscapes with cultivated gardens, and the construction of visual experiences that unite balance with uncertainty.

For the clients of the house on Rocca Way in Bel Air, I designed a landscape of outdoor rooms joined by a walking path. In the circumambulation of wilderness and cultivation, of moving sequentially through open and enclosed expanses, I wanted to encourage retreat, solitude, and meditation.

For two working artists in the industrial reality of Venice, I created a small-scale refuge that contrasts oasis and desert. Oasis was symbolized by a California pepper tree, wild *Liriope* var. and *Xyosia* var. grasses, and sweet-smelling gardenias; desert was represented by decomposed granite that also served as a stage for sculptures.

Rancho Dulce, our family citrus ranch in Ojai, has always been my experimental palette, allowing me the time and leisure to let ideas take shape in a situation that is under my control.

One noticeable threshold was where random growth met an organized frame. My thinking began with a series of concentric rings: the uncultivated mountains circling the orange groves—at the center of the rings, the house, surrounded by stone walls made of rocks from the mountains. To mark one edge of the property, we planted a row of poplar trees that is now seventy feet tall. Inside the garden, I negotiated the existing walls and dug new ones, often climbing the stairs to the second floor of the house to survey the spatial dynamic.

It was alchemical, this adding and removing of elements and my experimentation with native plants. Selecting the right materials and setting up a color palette began with careful attention to natural forces, like the year-round climate, soil, and wind conditions, and relative humidity. We wanted available plantings that were humble, not cranky, and able to perform dutifully and, essentially, to endure. Since at Rancho Dulce I am simultaneously the landscape architect and the client, I have been able to forge insights into both sides of the equation. As designer, I have certain ideas and intuitions about what can be done in the space. As client, I am more flexible and open to what seems to work and what doesn't. (I realize, too, sometimes I am impatient and my own worst critic.) Over the years, I have learned to take

1. House on Rocca Way, Bel Air, California, 1978

2

3

4

5

2-5. Rancho Dulce, Ojai, California

20

A. Millard Sheets Arts Complex
B. Entrance at Columbia Avenue
C. Quotations Walk
D. W. M. Keck Science Center

6

6. Scripps College Campus, drawing
depicts four landscape projects between
1993-2002
7. Quotations Walk, Scripps College,
Claremont, California, 1994

7

the pressure off by realizing that gardens are constantly evolving over time and that I always have the opportunity to edit and re-edit.

The Scripps College campus was especially compelling because it is the original site of the collaboration between Edward Huntsman-Trout, who created the landscape design, and Gordon Kaufmann, the architect. My overriding goal was to embrace and enhance their ideas. In Eckbo's 1964 book *Urban Landscape Design*, Huntsman-Trout wrote an essay that described the two axes of the Scripps campus. Along the east-west axis, the auditorium faces the Elm Tree Lawn and the Ellen Clark Revelle House (formerly the President's House), as well as distant views of Old Greyback, otherwise known as Mount San Gorgonio. Along the north-south axis, the Millard Sheets Art Center looks north toward the Bowling Green, the Eleanor Joy Toll Residence Hall, and the adjacent peaks of the Sierra Madre Mountains. For Huntsman-Trout, these axes made up the structural backbone of his plan, giving it strength and stability while contrasting with the free-form trees and the detailed planting of the courts and courtyards. There was a clear cross-axial diagram and a hierarchy of spaces in which the two main rectangles of lawn were lined with a series of ambiguous, smaller courtyards.

In order to connect the Garrison Theater and the Scripps Performing Arts Center (the music building) with W. M. Keck Science Center, we created a pedestrian link called Quotations Walk. In one direction along the walkway there are quotations about art by women scientists, and in the other direction are quotes by women artists about science. In the middle we created a garden room bordered by a fragment of the historical white-plaster boundary walls of the campus and an indented seat with planted, stepped access to the parking lot.

The projects in this chapter share multiple features of these early themes. The Bonhill Residence shows the importance of adopting a strong design that can accommodate changes over time. The Colton Avenue Streetscape for the University of Redlands was important for the way it helped to assimilate the campus with the surrounding community. The Cantitoe Farm project relied on ideas related to creating in-between, terraced garden rooms that could be inhabited. It continued the investigation of integrating hardscape with plant materials, merging architecture and landscape into a single endeavor. For the Ashley Ridge Residence, we focused on creating comfortable spaces for an active family, while for the Calabasas Civic Center we concentrated on building attractive, sustainable spaces for the community.

Bonhill Residence

Brentwood, California

My longest ongoing project is for a client whose house is perched on a hill overlooking the Westside of Los Angeles and has a thirty-foot grade change from the house to the bottom of the property. The goal was to turn the hilly terrain into a four-level garden linked by a stone stairway.

At the top, there is a level area for the house. The next level is for an office, another for the pool, while the bottom of the property is for two related gardens. The garden began with inspiration from writer Vita Sackville-West's celebrated Sissinghurst Castle Garden. From Sackville-West's tower, one can see two parallel hedges in the garden. The big idea was to link the house and the garden below by creating a stair paved with large chunks of stone. In the process, we cut the sloped hillside into two parts and created outdoor rooms that are bifurcated by two parallel hedges on either side of the path.

The hedges keep the view contained; one cannot see out until reaching the landings. At the third level there's an empty room and a full room. The full room was designed to be a citrus grove, but the soil wasn't suitable. It evolved into a sculpture garden with a wonderful garden folly designed by architect Michael Palladino. We planted *Wisteria* var. and grapes on the folly, and it has grown to become a shaded resting place.

A piece by artist Richard Long, called *Hollywood Circle*, fills a large circle with head-size boulders from the Four Corners area. The empty room became a badminton lawn set next to an early COR-TEN steel piece by Richard Serra; it is a beautiful space that is used, not just observed. I knew that over time there would be incremental additions, so the main diagram for the garden was designed to be strong and flexible enough to accommodate changes. We are constantly viewing and reviewing, putting in and taking out, while undergoing a wonderful process of discovery.

right: Hybrid Bermuda 'tifgreen' lawn forms the badminton court, contrasting with the surrounding Marathon sod.

opposite: The stone path leading away from the herb garden to the Richard Long piece

top: *Melaleuca amaryllis* frames
the front door.

bottom: From the teak deck, a view
of the terraces below

Site plan of Bonhill Residence
1 Parking court
2 Deck overlook
3 Office garden
4 Swimming pool
5 Badminton court
6 Axial stair and walk
7 Robert Therrien sculpture
8 Jenny Holzer bench
9 Circumambulatory path
10 Richard Serra sculpture
11 Row of pleached sycamores
12 Urn fountain
13 Richard Long sculpture
14 Rill
15 Fruit tree and herb garden

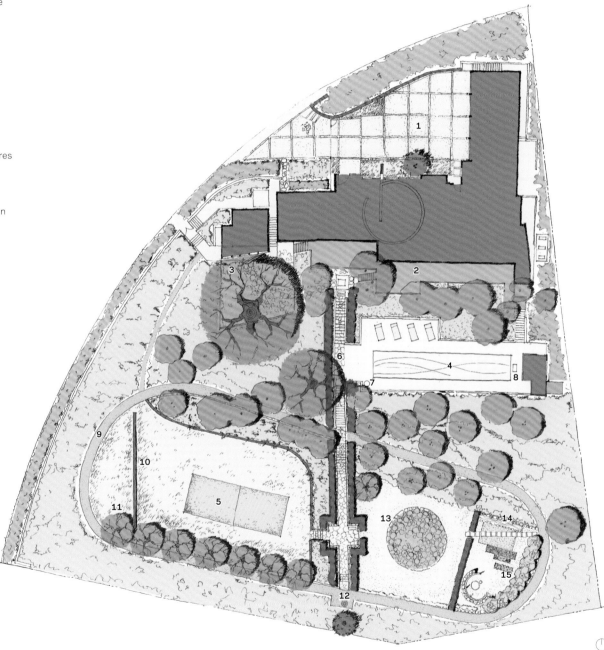

right: Circumambulatory walking path
crossing the axial stair

opposite: At the first landing, which
opens to the pool house and gym,
the slope is planted with paperbark and
sweetgum trees (*Melaleuca leucadendron*
and *Liquidambar styraciflua*).

opposite: The second landing intersects with the circumambulatory walking path.

top: In this view from the office garden, arboreal mass of the trees has filled in over the years.

bottom: A large urn fountain is situated at the terminus of the stair axis.

left: At the third level, there is a full
room and an empty room; this is the
empty room.

above: In the empty room, an early Richard
Serra COR-TEN steel sculpture remains
level while the earth around it slopes.

opposite: From the badminton court, the
sloping hedges of the stair axis are visible
behind the arboreal mass of the trees.

Overlook from the pool terrace and
view of the full room

Between the fruit tree and herb garden
and the axial stair is a sculpture by
Richard Long.

In the herb garden are a linear rill, potted
citrus trees, and a garden pavilion.

The garden pavilion is covered with
Wisteria and white Thompson seedless
grapes.

Colton Avenue Streetscape, University of Redlands

Redlands, California

The University of Redlands is located sixty miles east of downtown Los Angeles in an area that still maintains some of its rural past from the citrus groves surrounding the city. The campus needed to define itself better in relationship to the City of Redlands. Our primary contribution was to define the campus boundary by designing a gateway and to integrate Colton Avenue, which runs through the campus, with the rest of the university. In association with Meyer & Allen Associates, we turned it into a student-friendly campus drive with safe crossing points. Our goal was to establish gateways and streetscape planting that would reflect the tradition and graciousness of this small, historically important private university.

The city and university were required to upgrade the storm drainage system along Colton Avenue as well as run underground utilities and cables. Taking advantage of this required street construction, we proposed a center median on the avenue, which was planted with a hybrid of Mexican fan palms and California fan palms, as well as *Agaves* var., grasses, and succulents.

We created a planting edge between the curb and sidewalk on the north and south sides of the street. This city street runs right through the middle of the university; students cross it all the time. We widened the median and planted it with *Agaves* var. and other impenetrable plants so that students would not pass through and had to use the crosswalks with traffic signals. Parkways are planted with cork oaks trees and indigenous California fan palms, while pistache trees accent the sidewalk with scarlet-autumn color. The gateways are composed of limestone and ironwork walls planted with *Wisteria* var., an olive grove set in a field of *Iris* var., and beds of succulent plantings. Cobbled brick paving recalls the former Redlands' brick kilns located nearby. The result is a landscape that invites people to the campus, increases student safety, and clarifies its boundaries.

right: The student center with its water fountain

far right: Crape myrtles (*Lagerstroemia indica*) underplanted with *Abelia x grandiflora* form the border of the diagonal walk.

opposite: Looking down the median—at *Agaves*, blue oat grasses (*Helictotrichon sempervirens*), and red yuccas (*Hesperaloe parviflora*)—one can see the old Mexican and California fan palms (*Washingtonia robusta* and *Washingtonia filifera*), which were planted before the turn of the last century.

right: Typical street sections

below: Plan drawings of the Colton
Avenue Streetscape and the olive grove at
the campus entry

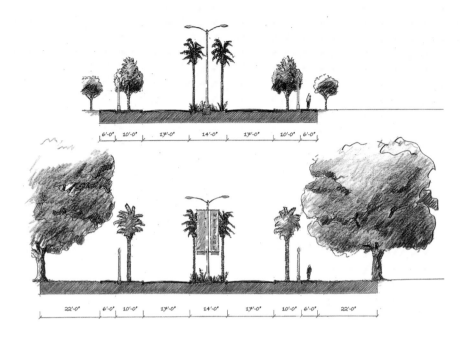

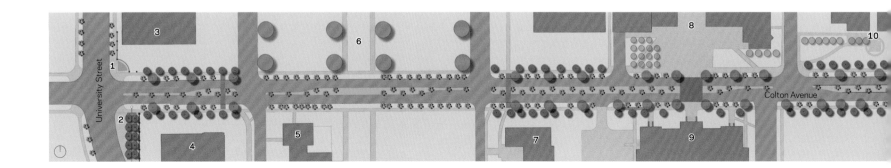

Built Elements
1 Monument wall and signage
2 Campus entry
3 Bekins-Holt Hall
4 Larsen Hall
5 Peppers Art Center
6 Quad framing the axis
   between the Administration
   Building and Memorial Chapel
7 Willis Center
8 University Center
9 Currier Gymnasium
10 Science Center
11 Historic Orchards

Landscape
A Olive grove and rill
B Median planting
C Hybrid fan palms
D Cork Oak Street trees
E Pistache Street trees
F Quad oaks

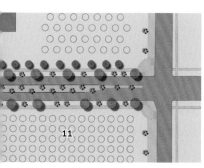

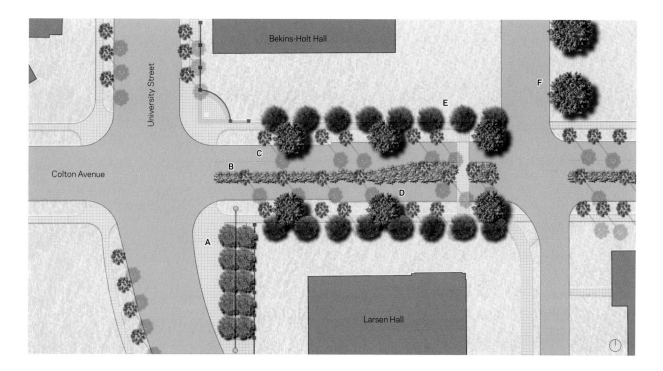

above: A low-spreading firethorn hedge (*Pyracantha hybrid 'Ruby Mound'*) encourages students to use crosswalks.

top right: Looking toward the chapel and quad, dwarf century plant (*Agave desmettiana*) and red yucca (*Hesperaloe parviflora*) are planted in the median that separates traffic lanes.

bottom right: View of the olive grove and monument at the campus entry

opposite: Hybrid fan palms (*Washingtonia filifera x robusta*) were planted in the new median.

Cantitoe Farm

Bedford, New York

Built in the 1870s as a rural farm surrounded by a deciduous forest, one hundred years later Cantitoe Farm was perched on a promontory in one of the most prestigious areas close to New York City. For a house sitting on top of a hill, with lawn sloping down on all sides, we proposed the creation of intermediate terraces that would be linked together. After studying the plan, I realized that it was necessary to build a series of retaining walls to create a series of terraces that could be used for entertaining, play, and relaxation.

A huge lawn cascaded down the hill but it was not usable space, and during the summer months it required large amounts of irrigation. I knew that significant grading and earth movement were necessary. We enlarged an existing meadow area to create an Icelandic pony track and used the excavated earth as fill for the new terraces. During construction, we ate outside and looked at the footings, mock-ups, and samples of paving and stairs. The client made major decisions about the landscape and enjoyed the process. I learned a great deal from our discussions.

There were highly talented Italian stone masons helping us to construct planted steps, using big curbs of blue stone measuring three feet (0.9 meters) long plus geometric pieces of stone that were eight feet (2.4 meters) by eight feet by eight inches (0.2 meters). The idea was to have geometric pieces mixed with the randomly shaped slabs. They worked for two days laying out the stones. The client didn't like it at all; he said it looked like a stealth bomber wing. I asked him to go to the bottom of the steps, look up, and imagine what it would look like when they were grown in. We designed a miniature apple orchard and a circular pond with a weeping willow tree, creating a beautiful and serene effect.

The landscape of Cantitoe Farm incorporates several design philosophies: Japanese principles concerning impermanent beauty and spiritual nourishment; Southern California modernist ideas about integrating landscape and architecture in a sensitive way; and the work of certain contemporary artists like Agnes Martin, whose paintings reveal the controlled beauty of repetition and proportion.

opposite: These steps are planted with two kinds of thyme (*Thymus pseudolanuginosus* 'Hall's Wooly' and *Thymus serpyllum* 'Reiter's Red'), low-spreading juniper (*Juniperus procumbens* 'Nana'), and oregano (*Oreganum rotundifolium* 'Kent Beauty').

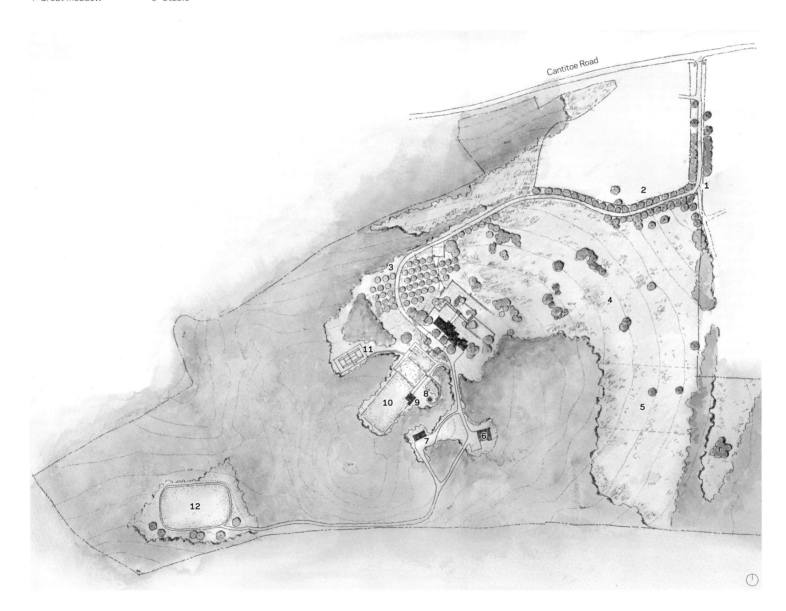

Site plan of Cantitoe Farm   5 Horse pasture   10 Dressage ring
1 Entry gate   6 Writer's studio   11 Tennis court
2 Allée   7 Tool shed   12 Icelandic horse track
3 Orchard   8 Water tower
4 Great meadow   9 Stable

Cantitoe Road

Detailed plan of the main
house and terraces
A Entry court
B Residence
C Kitchen garden

D Dining terrace
E Lawn steps to
croquet lawn
F Croquet lawn
G Weeping cherry terrace

H Planted steps
I Lawn steps to Meadow

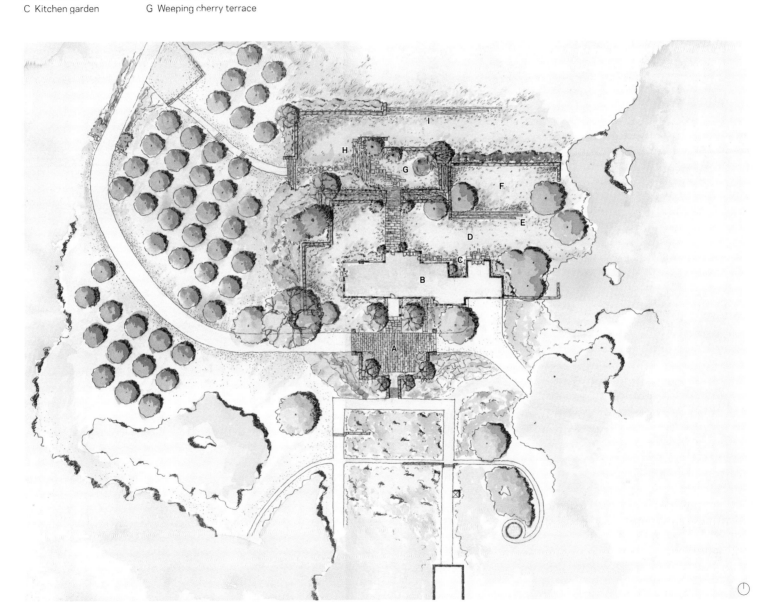

left: Bird's nest spruce (*Picen abies nidiformis*) and mugo pines (*Pinus mugo*) border the bottom landing of the planted steps.

above: A weeping Higan cherry tree (*Prunus subhirtella var. pendula*) is reflected in the circular pond, planted with Egyptian blue lilies (*Nymphaea*).

opposite: Honey locust trees (*Gleditsia triacanthos*) filter views from the approach to the house.

left: Thirty-inch thick masonry walls were built from local stone.

above: Planted steps connect the intermediate and lower terraces.

opposite: The steps are framed with Montgomery spruce (*Picea pungens glauca 'Montgomery'*), mugo pine (*Pinus mugo*), and bird's nest spruce (*Picea aibes 'Nidiformis'*).

left: View of the apple orchard from the house's main terrace; in the foreground are Eastern white pine trees (*Pinus strobus*), Japanese maples (*Acer palmatum*), Chinese junipers (*Juniperus chinensis*), and Japanese blood grass (*Imperata cylindrica 'Rubra'*).

opposite: On the planted steps, two shapes of blue stone were used: a stone plank and a large piece with a straight edge.

Ashley Ridge Residence

Hidden Hills, California

On a very rainy day, a couple with three active children came by our office on the recommendation of architect Lise Matthews, who was designing their residence in Hidden Hills. They wanted my help in making an estate in which every part was usable, with lots of places for their children to engage in sports. The first part of the design process was paring down the requirements to the essentials, streamlining the design, and establishing a budget. A circular driveway had been envisioned for the front, but we quickly realized that it was inefficient, given the steep slope. We created a welcoming experience by designing an allée of *Jacaranda* var. trees on both sides of the drive, which remained at the side of the house. A new pedestrian approach was constructed with a staircase that begins on center and a birch tree on the slope; it then shifts across the slope in a mid-landing terrace to realign and center itself on the front door. We decided to use a railing that is fanciful and looks like a vine. Some trees were removed, others were added, and the hillside was covered with layers of drought-tolerant shrubs, including *Teucrium* var., *Salvia* var., rosemary, lavender, and *Elaeagnus* var. The stairway became a gracious layered passage in which the experience of climbing is complemented by hidden rest areas.

The clients wanted to make every part of the garden functional, with both intimate and large seating areas, views, gardens, and places to play sports. The soil was so poor it looked like nothing would grow. We removed a guesthouse and additional structure to create a large soccer lawn bordered by a gravel path on all four sides. From the lawn, one ascends to the new pool area through a *Wisteria*-covered pergola. The pool and pool house were built on an upper pad that has become a center of activities. In the past, I have taken out numerous pool slides and never participated in putting one in. The clients showed me a picture of a slide that looked okay and turned out to be a great way to use the rest of the hillside. It is chartreuse green, like a giant tomato caterpillar, and is situated within a cluster of *Elaeagnus pungens* and redwood trees.

The garden complements the house to create a refuge and place of comfort for an active family. There are so many spaces to move about, plenty of cushioned chairs and couches, barbeques, and fountains on the lower and upper terraces. A row of crepe myrtle trees separates the main house and the pool house. The soccer quad and pool fit together with a vegetable garden, trampoline, tennis court, and orchard walk. It looks good and fits together in a well-proportioned way, while apparently random plantings and hidden spaces give it a taste of wabi-sabi.

opposite: A *Jacaranda* tree allée frames
the steep driveway up to the house.

Site plan of Ashley Ridge Residence
1 Entry gates
2 Entry stair
3 Terrace
4 Jacaranda allée

5 Vegetable garden and fruit trees
6 Cutting garden
7 Soccer lawn
8 Pergola
9 Croquet lawn

10 Fire pit
11 Pool pavilion
12 Pool and spa
13 Pool slide
14 Circumambulatory walkway

15 Equestrian path
16 Woodland garden
17 Sitting garden

left: Trees were relocated from the
back of the property to create filtered
views of the house.

above: View of the back of the house,
with a spectator bench next to the
soccer lawn

opposite: The stone stair ascends to a midlanding terrace that traverses the slope and then ascends once again to the front landing A sloping lawn was replaced with plantings of *Elaeagnus*, *Lavandula*, *Teucrium*, and coast rosemary (*Westringia fruticosa*).

right: Outside the library is a seating area and fountain.

opposite: A *Wisteria*-covered pergola separates the upper pool lawn from the soccer lawn below it.

top: New Zealand flax (*Phormium 'Yellow Wave'*) flanks the stairs leading from the pool to the soccer lawn.

bottom: A view of the main house from the upper pool lawn on a foggy day

top: View of the pool pavilion

bottom: California redwood trees (*Sequoia sempervirens*) and pepper trees (*Schinus molle*) are planted on the slope above the pool to form an enclosure.

opposite: A jacuzzi is set in the pool deck, while a fire pit with tree trunk seats are set in the lawn.

Calabasas Civic Center
Calabasas, California

When the city of Calabasas wanted to construct a formal and inviting municipal center and library, it chose Robert A.M. Stern as its design architect and Harley Ellis Devereaux as executive architects. The goal was to create a community hub where people can read books, use computers, conduct city business, and relax outdoors in a comfortable environment. Facing one another, the library and city hall form a civic plaza. Stern took inspiration from the Mediterranean-style architecture prevalent in early twentieth-century Southern California. These distinctive elements are evident in the towers, balconies, and arches of the buildings and public spaces. The refined, elegant pair of buildings is linked by a gently curving pergola planted with espaliered roses. The main idea for the project was to make the outdoor reading and eating areas and the civic plaza inviting by planting a grove of olive trees that recalls the area's agricultural past, in combination with large ash and cypress trees.

Calabasas is fifteen miles inland from Malibu. During the summer, ninety-degree temperatures are common. Sustainability was an important component of our design and the Civic Center is rated LEED Gold by the U.S. Green Building Council. Our goal was to focus on colorful and fragrant drought-tolerant plants and native and Mediterranean trees and shrubs. Skyline cypress trees punctuate the steps that rise up to the north plaza. The olive grove recalls the agricultural legacy of Calabasas and creates a shaded pedestrian-scaled space that complements the architecture of the library and city hall. The landscaped areas are irrigated using a highly efficient system that includes moisture sensors and low-water-use irrigation emitters.

Our challenge was to create a municipal landscape that met xeriscaping and local requirements while being attractive and appealing. At the beginning, the plan was to have three floors of parking below the entire area, which would necessitate planting on top of the concrete structure. Since we wanted to include a number of olive trees, we worked out a way to recess half of the planters on top of the structural columns. Halfway through the design process, the city decided to have parking only underneath the two buildings, which made it less expensive and gave us more flexibility. A small amphitheater was incorporated into the architecture of the library. The hardscape is set up to accommodate a larger amphitheater in the future, one that will be built into the bowl-shaped hillside that covers the back of the entire property.

opposite: Richly textured plant materials surround the back of the library, including dwarf fountain grass (*Pennisetum Alopecuroides 'Hameln'*) and the flowering shrubs Ambridge rose (*Rosa 'Auswonder'*) and autumn sage (*Salvia greggii*).

64

Site plan of Calabasas
Civic Center
1 Amphitheater
2 Arcade passageway
3 Rose garden

4 Stepped garden
5 Parking
6 Hillside planting

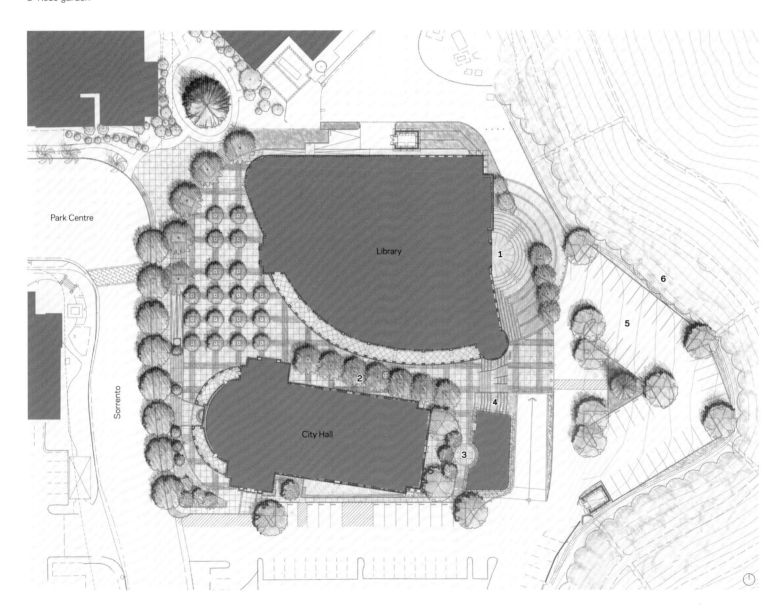

Park Centre

Sorrento

Library

City Hall

The civic center has a commanding
presence that creates a focal point within
the community.

Plantings include lamb's ears (*Stachys byzantina*),
Cleveland sage (*Salvia clevelandii 'Allen
Chickering'*), Mexican sage (*Salvia leucantha*),
and coast rosemary (*Westringia fruticosa*).

Outdoor seating fills the space
under the ash trees.

A straight line of raywood ash trees
(*Fraxinus oxycarpa 'Raywood'*) contrasts
with the curve of the arcade.

An olive grove provides shade at
the entry of city hall.

II. FIRE & WATER

1

2

3

Southern California is at the North American continent's edge. We face the beauty of the Pacific Ocean while watching out for the Santa Ana winds from the desert, which threaten firestorms, and worrying about possible earthquakes. It is a volatile mix and a dynamic meeting of geologic plates.

In the early 1980s, Harvard University invited twelve landscape architects to participate in the exhibition Transforming the American Garden: 12 New Landscape Designs. We were asked to design an entirely theoretical landscape, free to choose our client, site, and budget. Influenced by my home in the mountains above Malibu, I envisioned a retreat for scientists, theologians, and convicts; each personality represented an aspect of the human psyche: the empirical, the spiritual, and the irrational. Named *Hydrotopia*, meaning "place of water," it was a symbolic journey in which water running throughout the site represented the stream of consciousness.

Hydrotopia was to function as a refuge or retreat in which confrontation and discovery are achieved by synthesizing multiple elements. I view *Hydroptopia* as a series of suggestive fragments that can be brought together only by those who walk its ritual paths. The garden invites this circumambulation; for in a real sense, there is no destination other than exploration and self-discovery, through interlocking but noncohesive visual metaphors. In *Hydrotopia*, landscape becomes something more than a pretty garden. It functions like language; through its discontinuities, it uncovers deeper meanings within the mind.

A decade after creating *Hydrotopia*, a firestorm destroyed my mountain home, causing me to experience the profound ways in which nature rises, destroys, and then rises like a phoenix from the ashes. *Firestorm*, the conceptual piece, addresses these realities and celebrates the native foliage and plants that require fire for germination and survival. *Hydrotopia* used water as an image for the flow of the human psyche. *Firestorm* represented ashes and rejuvenation: seasonal times, like psychic times, of moisture, aridity, destruction, and rejuvenation.

All of the projects in this chapter are located within the native California chaparral and have water and the conservation of water as primary to their designs. The Palm Canyon Residence in Malibu is designed as a comfortable refuge for a large family; it incorporates a pepper tree allée, olive grove, and planted steps. The School of the Arts Plaza, for the University of California, Irvine project with Maya Lin has become a central meeting place as well as an exploration of our five senses. Red Tail Ranch relies ultimately on natural rainfall. Scenario Lane Residence juxtaposes native drought-resistant plants with local chaparral. The Santa Monica Public Library uses water as its primary metaphor and includes a fountain in the middle of the courtyard to provide relief from hot summer days; it is the focus of our efforts to create a sustainable landscape. Our design for the Industrial Complex in Santa Fe Springs also emphasizes the conservation of water.

1. *Hydrotopia*, site collage for Transforming the American Garden: 12 New Landscape Designs, Harvard University, 1988
2. *Hydrotopia*, circumambulatory path
3. *Hydrotopia*, mountain horizon collage
4. *Firestorm*, conceptual piece, 1993-4

March 1994:
This year spring has a meaning that I haven't experienced before. My house and the 130 acres I have lived on for the last fifteen years were transformed by the Malibu fires. Not only the experience of the fire, but its aftermath, has deeply affected me. The fire was so hot—3,000 degrees Fahrenheit, with 60 mph winds. There were four of us who stayed on the property until ten o'clock at night. We decided that only when we saw the flames at Big Rock would we depart. I thought I would see a small, red fringe outlining the mountain, because there were giant, billowing yellow clouds of smoke purged with black, illuminated far beneath. To my amazement, I saw the flame. It was a singular, 200-foot giant yellow tongue that arched overhead and touched the *Eucalyptus* tree next to me. When we were barely out of reach, I turned back to look. I was overwhelmed by the ferocious beauty of the fire as it ravaged and danced like a mythical animal with sinuous muscles.

A garden about ashes and the rejuvenation of root crowns sprouting brilliant red sumac leaves, and turquoise flesh inside the *Yucca* erupting like a fountain, is a garden about spring. The garden I would make would be a rectangular earthen room, the floors lined with hard-packed, blackened decomposed granite—aligned so that the sun would rise on the Vernal Equinox at its entrance. The path would be bordered on both sides with *Opuntia ficus-indica*, *Opuntia fragilis var. brachyclada*, and *Opuntia phaeacantha* with yellow spines. Spaced in a tight grid within the center of the room would be *Yucca* pineapples sprouting their goods. Intermingled, the random root crowns of the *Rhus laurina* would sing red all day long. At the end of this long, earthen room are two *Phoenix canariensis* palm trunks, blackened with soot, whose fronds at the top salute the insistence that nature will survive in grand style. The garden would be one of a new beginning, of the return of life after cataclysmic fire.

4

Palm Canyon Residence

Malibu, California

Living in Malibu, I have enjoyed a long and rewarding relation-ship with a large, extended family. For this project, I drew on landscape elements from a number of projects. At our place in Ojai, we have a small rectangle of native grasses surrounded by stone walls. At Scripps College, green lawns form large spaces that frame views of the surrounding Los Padres National Forest. For his own home in Santa Barbara, landscape architect Lockwood de Forest planted a green rectangle of kikuyu grass that became yellow in summertime and mirrored the golden hills. Adapting these ideas, I created a large rectangle of lawn to capture the views of the surrounding hills and nearby Franciscan retreat.

Situated within one of the canyons along the Malibu coast, the Malibu Fire of 1993 burned down to the back of the house. The main house is approached through an allée of mature California pepper trees, opening onto a parking court covered with decomposed granite. The front entry court is planted with broad-leaved tropical plants and succulents, whose openness recalls Honoré de Balzac's words, "If one looks at anything long enough, it becomes interesting."

The rectangle of grass is the center; things happen around its ambiguous edges. The buildings nestle into the landscape to surround the big, open lawn. Local masons were brought in to create stone walls that form the space; they also make the transitions between different grade changes. Local stone defines the edges of the great lawn. Stone walls slide past each other to frame planted steps. The idea was to create a viable and sustainable landscape within a compound designed to accommodate active children and their parents.

right: The decomposed granite parking court is planted with new and existing large pepper trees (*Schinus molle*) to provide shade.

opposite: Bouquet Canyon stepping stones define the great lawn.

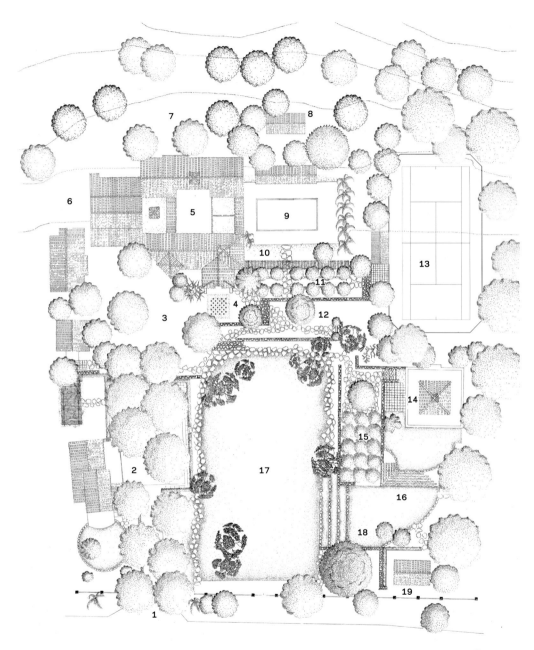

Site plan of Palm Canyon
Residence
1 Entry
2 Parking court
3 Entry court
4 Outdoor chess
5 Main house
6 Vegetable garden
7 Avocado grove
8 Gym and sundeck
9 Pool
10 Pergola
11 Purple plum allée
12 Iris Terrace
13 Tennis court
14 Pavilion
15 Olive grove
16 Planted steps
17 Great lawn
18 Lawn steps
19 Barn

top: The view to the front of
the house from across the entry court

bottom: Detail of the edge of
the great lawn

Lawn steps make the transition from
the great lawn to the olive orchard. Planted
along the stone wall, a Graham Thomas
'David Austin' rose (*Rosa 'David Austin'*)
borders the orchard.

above: Blooms of a silk floss tree
(*Chorissa speciosa*) have fallen next to
the outdoor chess game.

opposite: An opening in the purple plum
allée presents a view to the great lawn.

From the sunroof of the gym, the great lawn can be seen beyond the pool and surrounding pergola.

Dry mortar stone walls separate the purple plum allée from the pool area's pergola.

Planted steps at the pavilion.

School of the Arts Plaza, University of California, Irvine

Irvine, California

When Maya Lin was asked to create the Claire Trevor School of the Arts plaza for the University of California, Irvine, she knew she wanted to collaborate with a landscape architect on the West Coast. Lin came to our office and saw that we like to build models, which helped convince her that we could work well together. It turned out to be a comfortable and creative seven-year, bicoastal collaboration.

Our mission was to transform an impersonal 30,000-square-foot (9,144-square-meter) area crisscrossed by three pedestrian walkways and surrounded by eight buildings, each designed by a different architectural firm, into a unified focal point for the entire campus. The administration wished to convert a network of pedestrian pathways into an arts plaza that would serve as a central meeting area. The goal was to take a group of forgettable, concrete-lined walkways between the buildings that house various arts programs and turn them into a gathering space and modestly designed outdoor performance venue. Ultimately built for $3.6 million, the arts plaza gives greater prominence to the Claire Trevor School of the Arts and by extension provides a new center of gravity on the north side of campus. At once an outdoor gallery, performance space, classroom, and park, the arts plaza sets the stage for multiple personal and social interactions.

One architecture critic noted that designing a plaza is among the toughest and most thankless jobs an architect can tackle. The public spaces that tend to work most effectively also tend to be the ones where the designer must be willing not only to forgo recognizable formal gestures but also to allow contingency to play a leading part. The edges of the planted rectangles of herbs and flowers, the grove of various sizes of sycamore trees, the orange trees at each entrance, the low walls crisscrossing the amphitheater, and the water table are each sharply defined, but their edges melt into the surrounding spaces of the plaza.

We collaborated on the site design. Creating the plaza with Lin involved making a terraced lawn out of an unused slope and installing a white, reflective painted wall that can be used as a projection surface for an outdoor amphitheater. This outdoor theater references the work of photographer Hiroshi Sugimoto and his photos of blank drive-in movie screens.

The design as a whole is organized around the five senses. Fragrant orange trees stand as sentries to entry points; native California sycamore trees evoke memories of the California plein-aire painters; a twenty-foot-wide fire lane has been planted with scent-exuding ground covers framed by concrete walkways for students as well as fire trucks; and whispering benches and video monitors relay audio and visual transmissions. Planting twenty-seven California sycamores, thirteen Mexican sycamores, and nine Valencia orange trees created much-needed shade during the summer. Lin's granite table subtly shimmers with a layer of water that slides across the surface, inviting touch, while her whispering benches produce a low hum.

opposite: View of amphitheater and the
Beall Center for Art and Technology

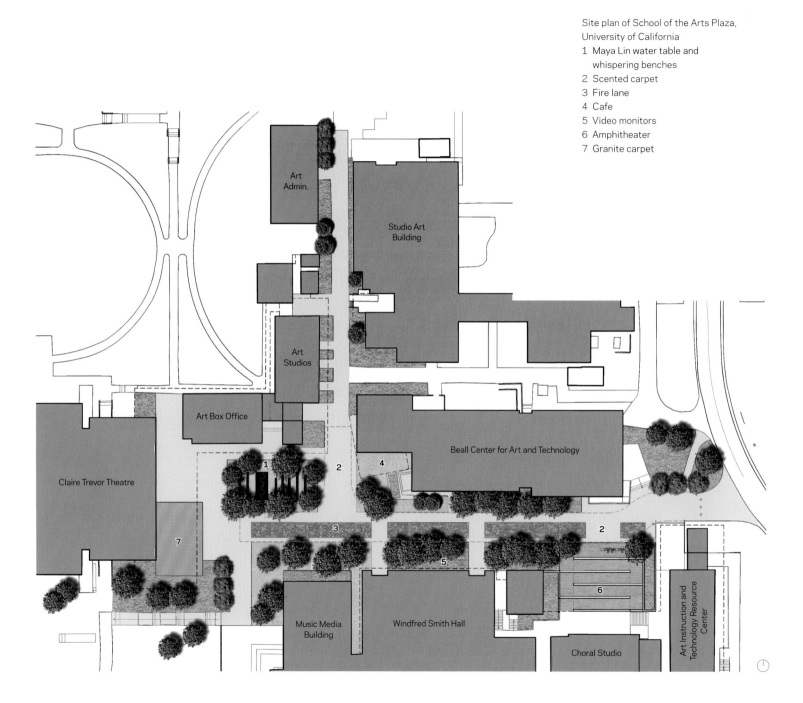

Site plan of School of the Arts Plaza,
University of California
1 Maya Lin water table and
   whispering benches
2 Scented carpet
3 Fire lane
4 Cafe
5 Video monitors
6 Amphitheater
7 Granite carpet

top: A newly planted grove of mixed-size California sycamore trees (*Platanus racemosa*) unity the walkway.

bottom: The outdoor classroom next to the fire lane

above: California sycamore trees
(*Platanus racemosa*) provide shade in
the outdoor study area.

top right: View down the length of the
plaza from the Claire Trevor Theater

bottom right: Scented carpet and fire lane

opposite: View of the amphitheater
and painted projection screen

top: Students walking on the scented carpet of pennyroyal (*Mentha pulegium*), thyme (*Thymus vulgaris*), oregano (*Origanum vulgare*), and snow-in-summer (*Cerastium tomentosum*)

bottom: The Fine Arts Plaza is paved with decomposed granite, concrete, and scented carpet.

opposite: Skateboarding is better on concrete.

Scenario Lane Residence

Bel Air, California

When a young couple in the entertainment industry decided to renovate an existing home overlooking the Stone Canyon Reservoir in Bel Air, they were faced with a number of challenges, not least of which was that the property is located on an elongated ridge with vertical drops on all sides. The husband had lived in the house for ten years before he met his wife. It was in an isolated location off the neighborhood of Beverly Glen with an awesome view of Stone Canyon Reservoir, but there was no place to park cars, the driveway was narrow, and the wife was afraid of stairs!

We were called in to make the property safe for children and resistant to fire. At the same time, we were asked to take advantage of the site's views to create a dramatic landscape that worked both with the renovated house and with a new studio building designed by Michael Palladino of Richard Meier & Partners Architects. We decided to take advantage of the views and topography by creating a landscape that unfolds through a cinematic-like series of outdoor rooms that serve as refuges and viewpoints. One enters the property at the end of a rustic road with a tall rock outcropping on one side and a precipitous hillside on the other. This area has been planted heavily to compress the views. There is a path to walk on made from six-inch stones with plants in between, but one can also drive on it to reach the new car port.

A second outdoor room reveals itself as one walks along the driveway, which has been tinted to match the color of the stone found throughout the site. Several large outcroppings of Chico conglomerate rock found on the property were the inspiration for a series of faceted sandstone walls that mediate between the existing and new architectural elements. Steps negotiate between the rocks and the hillside. They are planted with dwarf olive, lavender, blue oat grass, and sages.

There are very steep stairs up to the entrance, and a second set of stairs from the house to the studio. A lap pool appears to cantilever off the edge of the house. A lawn area at the top of the property provides a safe play area for the couple's young child. Terraced planting areas adjacent to the lawn provide a space for a cultivated inner sanctum made up of citrus trees and a garden with vegetables and herbs used for cooking.

The big idea was to incorporate native California plant materials that weave in and out from the banks of the hillsides into the more cultivated garden areas in the middle of the property, adjacent to the living spaces. The planting palette consists of Mediterranean-zone ground covers, shrubs, and trees close to the structures mixed with drought-tolerant California natives that blend with the adjacent chaparral. Several coast live oak trees will, over time, punctuate the outdoor spaces and add another cadence to the sequence of gardens and views. Our goal was to make the complicated series of stairs and vertical layering that connected the different areas of the house appear effortless. Outdoor rooms, borrowed landscapes, and the use of multiple viewpoints enlarge the usable area and enhance the feeling of open space while preserving a comfortable refuge in the center of the property.

opposite: A mix of sage (*Salvia 'Allen Chickering'*), dwarf olive (*Ole a europaea 'Little Ollie'*), and lavender (*Lavendula heterophylla*) line the steps to the upper and lower entrance to the studio.

Site plan of Scenario Lane Residence

1 Stone Canyon Reservoir
2 Parking court
3 Fire pit
4 Drivable walkway
5 Pool
6 Front entry
7 Planted steps
8 Rock outcropping
9 Main house
10 Studio
11 Terrace
12 Master bedroom terrace
13 Fruit tree and herb terrace
14 Upper meadow

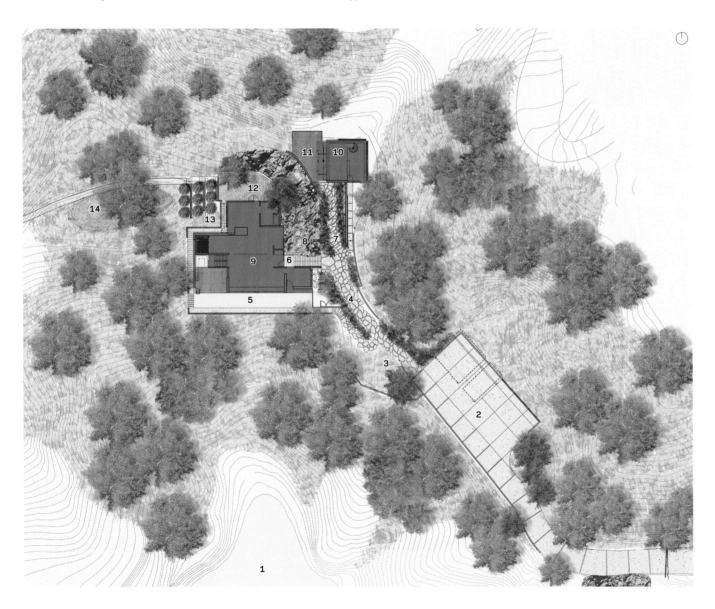

88

Large stone pavers are interplanted with bishop's weed (*Aegopodium podagraria 'Variegatum'*), silver carpet (*Dymondia margaretae*), coral bells (*Heuchera*), and pennyroyal (*Mentha pulegium*).

The house overlooks Stone Canyon Reservoir and is placed within a planting palette of native and Mediterranean materials.

Landscape timbers form citrus tree and herb terraces that lead to the upper meadow, and gravel troughs facilitate drainage.

The master bedroom terrace is planted with coast live oak (*Quercus agrifolia*).

The upper meadow overlook is planted with creeping
red fescue (*Festuca rubra*), native douglas iris (*Iris
douglasiana*), and manzanita (*Arctostaphylos 'Sunset'*).
Century City can be seen in the distance.

opposite: Morning sunrise illuminates the existing
blue gum tree (*Eucalyptus globulus*).

above: The path descends toward a vista overlooking
the reservoir, with a drought-tolerant mix of sage (*Salvia
'Allen Chickering'*), lavender (*Lavandula heterophylla*),
and blue oat grass (*Helictotrichon sempervirens*).

right: The fire pit area is planted with bridal wreath
(*Francoa ramosa*), coffee berry (*Rhamnus californica
'Eve Case'*), and coast rosemary (*Westringia fruticosa*),
and features a scented carpet of mother of thyme
(*Thymus praecox*) and pennyroyal (*Mentha pulegium*).

Santa Monica Public Library

Santa Monica, California

I have worked extensively with Moore Ruble Yudell Architects & Planners, beginning with my collaboration with Buzz Yudell on a garden for Charles Jencks and Maggie Keswick.

Since our firms have worked on so many projects together and we are both located in Santa Monica, we were pleased when John Ruble asked us to work with them on the Santa Monica Public Library project. It was a nourishing experience in which, throughout the process, we collaborated and contributed our insights and perspectives. In creating this design, we employed the metaphor of illuminating a world beneath the surface. Santa Monica is the city by the bay—the large, shimmering body of water at the edge of the North American continent, reflecting the sky. In order to see the underwater topography and the world beneath the ocean, one needs to find some way to venture below the surface. In the same way, the Santa Monica Public Library reveals the depths of human knowledge and cultures; it allows us to look beneath the surface of everyday life to investigate the richness of our cultures.

Working with the architects, as well as artist Carl Cheng, our goal was to create an environment that would utilize sustainable measures to meet LEED Gold requirements. The on-grade parking lot was designed without curbs surrounding the planting areas to encourage drainage from the pavement into the planters, cleaning the stormwater runoff before it enters the city's storm drain system. Rooftops tilt toward the courtyard; rainwater is collected into downspouts and captured in a 200,000-gallon cistern below the building's subterranean parking. Water is filtered then pumped up from the cistern exclusively to irrigate the drought-tolerant materials planted throughout the entire site. The landscape design reinforces the civic quality of the library through a series of courtyards and midblock passageways that weave together the interior and exterior spaces as well as provide links with the city. The courtyards are designed to accommodate a wide range of activities, including small group discussions and larger gatherings and celebrations. A cafe space with outdoor seating activates the Central Court, which is the main garden of the library.

opposite: A staircase descends to the courtyard and to a bridge over a water feature that leads to the cafe, where a canopy creates shadows evoking underwater sea life.

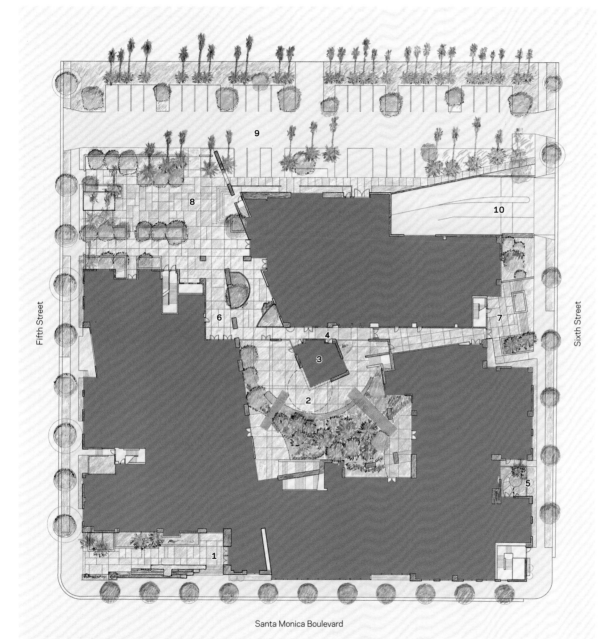

Site plan of Santa Monica
Public Library
1 Entry court
2 Main courtyard
3 Cafe
4 Paseo
5 Children's reading garden
6 Reception court
7 East entrance court
8 North entrance court
9 Parking court
10 Parking garage entry

top: Diagram showing how rain is collected from roofs into a 200,000-gallon cistern beneath the third floor of the garage

bottom: Night view of the front entry of the library at the corner of Santa Monica Boulevard and Sixth Street. Terraced plantings support the handicap ramp.

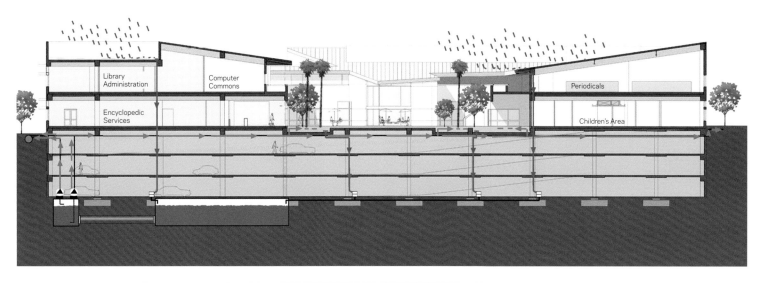

above: The setting sun illuminates the
patio terrace.

right: The two-inch-deep water feature is
lined with silicone carbonate that sparkles
as it wraps around the patio.

left: The Santa Monica Boulevard streetscape includes plantings of ponytail palm (*Beaucarnea recurvata*), fox tail *Agave* (*Agave attenuata*), and ground morning glory (*Convolvulus mauritanicus*).

right: The children's courtyard has a mound that is used as seating at story time.

above: Courtyard bubble planters are filled
with succulents and shoestring *Acacia* trees
(*Acacia stenophylla*).

right: The auditorium entrance is paved with
recycled glass. The planters contain yellow wave flax
(*Phormium 'Yellow Wave'*), yellow *Lantana* (*Lantana camara*), California pepper trees (*Schinus molle*),
and the saved palm trees.

opposite: Terraced planting of yellow torch aloe
(*Aloe arborescens 'Lutea'*) and dragon trees (*Dracaena drago*) form a lower entry court for the library.

Red Tail Ranch

Santa Ynez Valley, California

We collaborated with Frederick Fisher and Partners on a hilltop, wind-swept residence in the Santa Ynez Valley, above the city of Santa Barbara. The project is located in a paradigmatic California landscape of golden rolling hills and oak trees. The home includes a large painting studio and an office. It was clear to me that the shape of the land lent itself to a very appropriate metaphor. The house was going to sit on the land, like a saddle, with the ridge running through it like the backbone of a horse. The project became an exercise in restraint, letting the house recline comfortably into the landscape and become part of the mountains.

The entrance drive zigzags up the hill; driving round a sharp turn, one sees the house within a layering of shadows caused by existing oak trees and the canyon. Coming out of the shadows into the light, one sees the house across the canyon—a beautifully crafted object. We spent much of the time looking at the oaks on the property and at the natural drainage. There were two kinds of oaks: valley oaks and live oaks. We studied their locations in order to emulate the natural landscape while planting a minimum number of additional trees to accomplish specific tasks. There had to be a specific reason for adding each one. They had to serve a purpose and fit into the existing landscape.

We put in a path that led south, along the spine of the ridge, past the house and lap pool, down to a sunset-viewing bench. The entrance drive and paths were carefully orchestrated so that the approach and movement through the minimalist courtyard would highlight the lone, majestic live oak tree at its center. By careful planting, we created a series of shadows and visual thresholds through which the house can be viewed. Recalling the outdoor scrims of artist Robert Irwin, we created subtle interventions that allow one to savor the stunning environment. To create an elegant and effective landscape, the goal was to introduce the minimum number of trees to blend the graded slopes into the rolling hills.

right: View of the house from the path above

opposite: Mexican feather grass (*Nassella tenuissima*) flanks the backbone path leading to the house.

104

Site plan of Red Tail Ranch 5 Parking court
1 Entry gate   6 Vegetable garden
2 Oak threshold   7 Oak courtyard with fountain
3 Driveway   8 Backbone path
4 Spiral moon garden   9 Lap pool

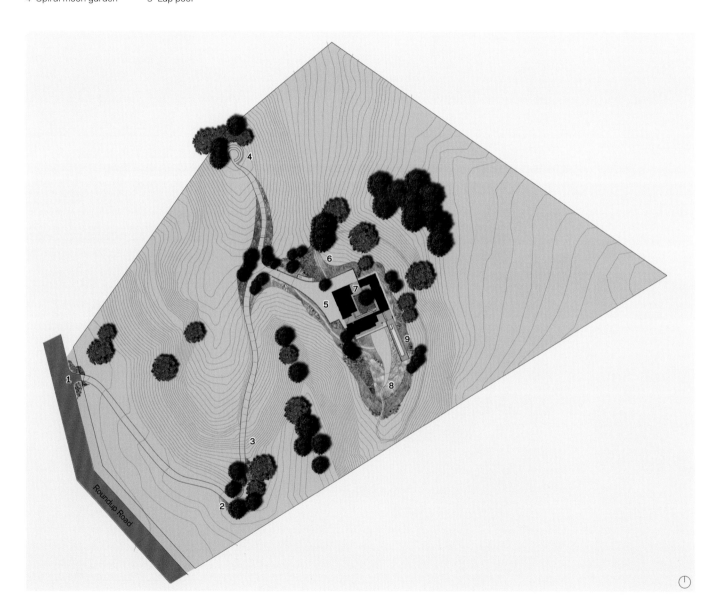

top: The placement of new oaks emulates the existing disposition of oak trees.

bottom: Deer grass (*Muhlenbergia rigens*), toyon (*Heteromeles arbutifolia*), and sage (*Salvia 'Allen Chickering'*) merge with views of the distant mountains.

In the courtyard, one multitrunk live oak
(*Quercus agrifolia*) provides shade,
while a carefully placed boulder is ready
to hold rainwater.

Wind ripples the water in the courtyard
fountain.

left: Water flows over the bronze spillway into a pebble-lined basin that aligns with the front entry.

above: A special eight-tine large rake was commissioned to maintain the courtyard gravel.

opposite: A COR-TEN steel frame and the dining terrace visually connect with the pool and views of the mountain horizon in the distance.

The spa and pool are set at a lower level than the dining terrace, which extends from the house.

Gulf muhlygrass (*Muhlenbergia capillaris*)
and sage (*Salvia 'Allen Chickering'*) fuse
with the existing landscape

Santa Fe Industrial Complex

Santa Fe Springs, California

When we were asked by Steven Ehrlich Architects to collaborate on the masterplan and site expansion for a supplier to large industrial and commercial facilities worldwide, we decided (as in our previous projects) to emphasize water conservation. The big idea for the thirty-six-acre site was to develop activity nodes and gardens outside the main corridors of the building. Working closely with the architects, we developed these areas to draw employees to cafe spaces, relaxation rooms, and other activities. These nodes offer alternative gathering spots in shaded and sunny areas. Along the main interior corridor of the buildings, or "Fork-Lift Alley," we used timber bamboo, fishtail palms, and other low-light-tolerant plant materials to frame and break up the spaces located under the skylights.

Outside of the building, we refurbished existing gardens, created new gardens, and converted existing parking into car courts with bioswale medians to catch and clean stormwater. Trees within these courts reduce reflective heat and create a shaded environment for staff and visitors. From the beginning of the design process, we took a proactive approach to encourage sustainable factors, striving to produce a landscape that is not only beautiful but also environmentally responsible. Bioswales were created by eliminating curbs surrounding the parking islands. An efficient drip-irrigation system was used, as well as an irrigation controller that utilizes weather information from satellites and moisture sensors in the planting areas. Rainwater was directed to planters filled with cobbles, grasses, and water-tolerant shrubs. Percolation into these planters reduces the load on the storm drain and helps to clean the water prior to it entering the system.

We participated in efforts to balance the amount of cut-and-fill soil by designing a series of berms (or constructed mounds) at the south edge of the site. These help to screen the parking areas from the street, and they provide open space for the perimeter pathway. The berms are planted with ornamental grasses, such as *Stipa*, *Pennisetum*, and *Festuca glauca,* as well as *Ceanothus*, lion's tail, dwarf bottlebrush, and kangaroo paw.

A circumambulatory path provides access to parking lots and lunchtime exercise around the entire property. The path is made of permeable decomposed granite that connects new fitness stations and a protected walk for employees. In a highly industrial neighborhood, filled with concrete tilt-up buildings set in oceans of asphalt and lawn, this property is planted with a wealth of noninvasive, Mediterranean plant materials that require less irrigation water.

opposite: A circumambulatory path winds around the entire thirty-six acre parcel. The noninvasive Mediterranean plant materials are labeled so that employees can learn their names.

114

Site plan of Santa Fe Industrial Complex
1 Main entrance
2 Guest parking
3 Dining courts

4 Interior gardens / "Fork-Lift Alley"
5 Activity node
6 Tree canopy to provide shade at
  southern exposure

7 Flush curbs and bioswales
8 Tree canopy to shade the parking lots
9 Landforms to balance the cut and fill
10 Walking path around site

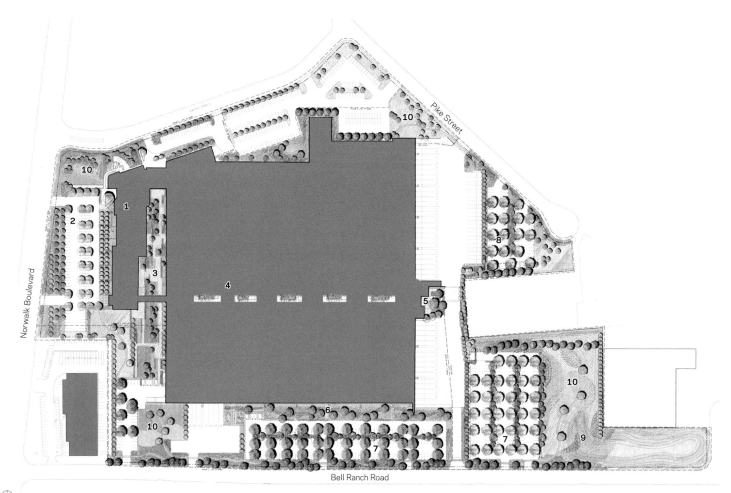

Section diagram of the site (top) and
an axonometric (bottom) illustrate the
project's sustainable characteristics.

Street | Jog / Walk Path | Parking Stall | Traffic Aisle | Parking Stall | Bioswale | Parking Stall | Traffic Aisle | Entry Garden | Fork-Lift Alley Spine | Interior Garden Node

Sustainability

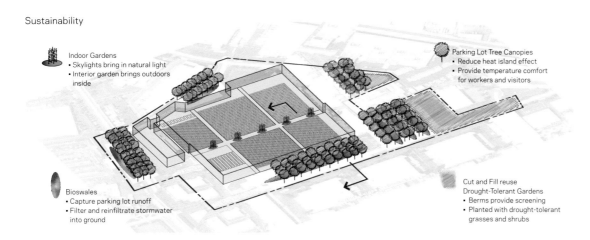

Indoor Gardens
• Skylights bring in natural light
• Interior garden brings outdoors inside

Parking Lot Tree Canopies
• Reduce heat island effect
• Provide temperature comfort for workers and visitors

Bioswales
• Capture parking lot runoff
• Filter and reinfiltrate stormwater into ground

Cut and Fill reuse
Drought-Tolerant Gardens
• Berms provide screening
• Planted with drought-tolerant grasses and shrubs

top: Existing *Jacaranda* trees were maintained, with low-water-use *Festuca glauca* as the ground cover.

bottom: Contrasting ground covers of *Senecio mandraliscae* and Mexican feather grasses (*Nassella tenuissima*) are in the foreground.

top: A third activity node incorporates outdoor seating for relaxation and conversation.

bottom. One of the activity nodes is an outdoor dining area that encourages people to go outside for casual lunches.

The grading plan for the project balanced
the cut and fill on-site.

Working with civil engineers, we designed
the parking lot with flush curbs to assist
stormwater flow into bioswales.

Layers of plants frame an entry to the building, including clumping giant bamboo (*Bambusa oldhamii*), Mexican feather grass (*Nassella tenuissima*), silk tree (*Albizia julibrissin*), rosemary (*Rosmarinus officinalis 'Lockwood de Forest'*), and New Zealand flax (*Phormium tenax 'Rubrum'*) in the background.

III. RECENT WORK

1

2

1-2. Installation, Cornerstone Festival of
Gardens, Sonoma, California, 2003

Working with private clients, I focus not only on what makes them comfortable, but also what will give their gardens a resonance that endures. Gardens have changing sets of references and memories, which turn them into catalysts for emotional experiences.

Author Tony Hiss writes about "simultaneous perception," which is when a landscape instills feelings of welcome, safety, wonder, and exhilaration. Over time, as I have become increasingly interested in issues of sustainability, I have also become less anxious to control and more interested in merging projects harmoniously with the natural environment.

In 2003, I was asked to be part of the Cornerstone Festival of Gardens in Sonoma, California, which showcases the work of landscape designers from around the world. We were each given a quarter-acre site to work with as we wished. I chose to turn the idea inside out (or upside down) by emphasizing the geological layering—the source of all of our projects. The earth is the largest living organism on the planet, and I wanted to make it the centerpiece of the installation. An excavated, inclined plane invited visitors to descend beneath ground level to the coolness of a water garden. Making the journey downwards encouraged participants to engage in a walking meditation and to smell, feel, touch, and breathe. The basic elements were packed earthen walls; Mexican feather grass; mulch of finely shredded redwood bark; a water feature planted with yellow water lilies; and, surrounding the excavation, large straw bales with steel straps and rebar pounded through to anchor and stabilize them. The water bar at the bottom drew the viewer near, with its sparkling reflections and flashes of gold fish.

Some projects evolve over time and require flexibility, patience, and rethinking. When artist John Baldessari decided to fix up his California bungalow, he chose to begin with the garden. At this period I was captivated and inspired by the work of the Mexican writer Octavio Paz, in particular his *A Tale of Two Gardens: Poems from India 1952–1995*, the two gardens being Mexico and India. We can have two gardens, I thought. I wanted to make every square inch of the property usable and to give Baldessari a place to go outside and relax. We set about screening off the neighbors, setting up interior views, and creating a series of three terraces. For the existing lower terrace around the house, we planted two California pepper trees and hung a hammock between them. The middle terrace contained a huge prickly pear cactus that became the centerpiece of a succulent garden, such as one would find in Mexico.

3

ELEMENTS

PACKED
RAMMED
EARTH WALLS

EARTH FUR
NASSELA
TENUISSMA

FIR MULCH
FINELY SHREDDED
REDWOOD BARK
4" DEEP

WATER BAR
BLACK
20 ML LINER
STONE SHARDS
AT BOTTOM

STRAW BALES
WITH STEEL
STRAPS 3" WIDE X
36" WITH HOLES
FOR NO. 3 REBAR
POUNDED THRU
TO ANCHOR &
STABILIZE

ASCENDING
DESCENDING
TRAVERSING
RESTING

RAMPS   CADENCE
STEPS   RATIO
         GRADIENT

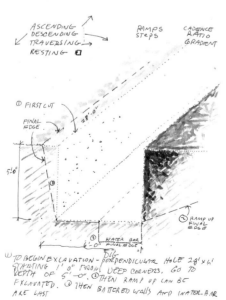

① FIRST CUT

FINAL
EDGE

28'-0"

5'-0"

RAMP UP
FINAL EDGE

WATER BAR
FINAL EDGE

DIG

① TO BEGIN EXCAVATION - PERPENDICULAR HOLE 28' X 6'
STARTING 1'-0" FROM DEEP CORNERS. GO TO
DEPTH OF 5'-0". ② THEN RAMP UP CAN BE
EXCAVATED. ③ THEN BATTERED WALLS AND WATER BAR
ARE LAST

4   5

3-5. Sketches of installation, Cornerstone
Festival of Gardens

6

7

8

9

The uppermost garden is reached by rock stairs leading to an olive grove brought to life with red brick mulch.

While the backspace was monochromatic with succulents and olives, the front was much more exuberant. We layered it with a series of turn-of-the-century colors, planting rosemary to cascade over a retaining wall on the property line, which borders a sidewalk that is considered a historical landmark. We planted canna lilies with striped, vibrant colors, as well as yellow and orange roses. We screened the telephone pole in front of the house with junipers, and Baldessari painted his front door bright orange.

Paring down the landscape to its essence, with a clear hierarchy of spaces, simplifies the overall structure and can be complemented by a rich palate of plant materials. La Mesa Residence integrates a series of small courts with their adjacent spaces: library, dining, study, and living. At the Yahoo Center, we brought to life an office complex by enhancing and rethinking its context. Malibu Beach House is a showcase for merging sustainability with aesthetic verve. At the East Fork Residence, we anchored the house to structural terraces planted with flowering crab apples and created veils of native trees through which to view the house. At Happy Canyon Residence in Santa Ynez, we refurbished and revitalized parts of a previous landscape to make it animated and built a new pond for fire flow. In Brazil, we created multiple refuges for office workers and the public. In all of this work, our intention was to create layers of discovery and experience.

10

6–10. Garden for John Baldessari: site sketch; upper olive grove terrace; view from the succulent terrace; view toward the large prickly pear cactus; view of the front of the house

La Mesa Residence

Santa Monica, California

La Mesa Drive in Santa Monica is lined by Moreton Bay fig trees that overlook the Riviera Country Club. We worked with architect Michael Hricak to design gardens, terraces, and retaining walls for a new house, with a full basement, situated on a hillside.

The two-story house rests on three levels. The entry level can be viewed as a series of four courtyards that serve as the framework for the house and blend the architecture with the site, carving out spaces through extraction. They integrate the architecture with the site in one continuous flow, from outside to inside and from inside to outside. Courtyards include the Living Court, the Study Court, the Dining Court, and the Reading Court. The public spaces open onto outdoor, shaded viewing gardens or expansive terraces for entertaining. The small-scaled courtyard gardens are tailored to the needs of the adjacent interior spaces; views into these intimate gardens come only in quick glimpses.

The large entry courtyard encompasses the drive, entrance walk, and garden. Integration of site and architecture begins with these elements, which are formed by lines of concrete paving that run parallel, rather than perpendicular, to the house and street. The paving blurs the thresholds between driveway, entrance walk, and the grasses planted in front of the house. The entrance becomes layers of planting with interspersed paving. The house is entered through a break in a stone wall, which leads into a courtyard filled with ferns and California sycamore trees. Sounds of the rustling sycamores mingle with the bubbling springs at the base of another

stone wall. Along this path, leading to the house's entrance, you can catch glimpses of smaller gardens.

We took great care with subtle details that display expert craftsmanship, and we used natural materials in unexpected and sometimes whimsical ways. Examples include: the wooden bridge, clasped together with stainless steel elements; stone turned on end to create a finely textured surface with planted joints; and similar plant materials with subtle variations in height and color that are placed adjacent to one another to heighten their differences.

We wanted to maintain unencumbered sightlines of the Riviera Country Club and Santa Monica Mountains from the main lawn terrace. The rectangular swimming pool is enclosed in the L-shaped courtyard and is on the upper level of the property. From there, four terraces go down the slope to an olive grove. We accentuated the quality of light and shadow by placing plant materials adjacent to walls, taking advantage of the changing sun exposures. One space leads to another, with only subtle clues to tell you what lies ahead. The width and materiality of each path changes. There are no straight routes; you must change course as you move through it.

Our client's impeccable taste and refined sensibilities added a great deal to the design process. Things were carefully considered, many full-scale mockups were made, and as a result there was a real sense of adventure and collaboration. The formality and minimalist quality to the house and garden are balanced by a sense of warmth, whimsy, and an attention to the smallest details of the design.

opposite: View from the sitting garden showing the layering of sycamore trees behind black fountain grass (*Pennisetum alopecuroides 'Moudry'*)

126

Site plan of La Mesa Residence
1 Existing Moreton Bay fig trees
2 Driveway and walk
3 Sitting garden
4 Entrance court

5 Rill
6 Study court
7 Dining court
8 Living court
9 Reading court

10 Lawn steps
11 Pool
12 Parterre garden
13 Sycamore terrace
14 Library terrace

15 Spa terrace
16 Olive walk
17 Lower meadow

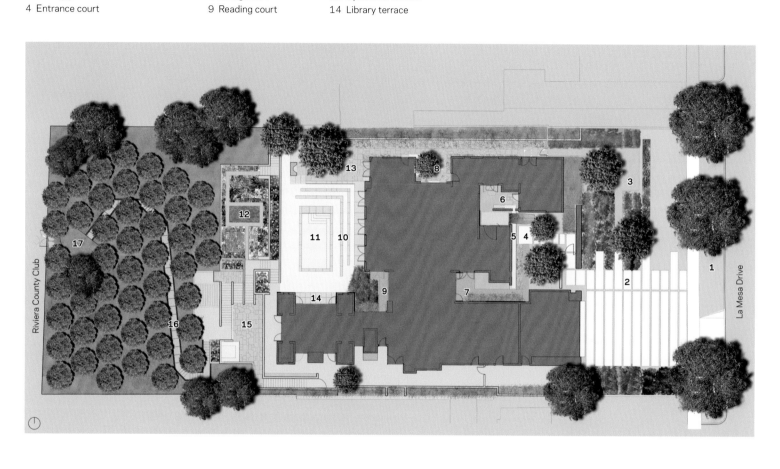

Riviera County Club

La Mesa Drive

top: The driveway and walkways are
treated as a single layered surface
with strips of grass between each band.
Flush runway lights demarcate the
pedestrian entrance.

bottom: A decomposed granite path
leads from the entrance to a small
semiprivate sitting garden. Plantings
include white lavender (*Lavandula
angustifolia 'Alba'*), black fountain grass
(*Pennisetum alopecuroides 'Moudry'*)
and California sycamore trees (*Platanus
racemosa*).

Inside the courtyard, concrete pads lead through mother ferns (*Asplenium viviparum*) and white camellias (*Camellia*). A wooden bridge crosses over a linear water feature (the rill) for arrival at the front door.

The dining court looks out onto a glass-enclosed stairwell next to a Japanese maple (*Acer palmatum*) and mother ferns (*Asplenium viviparum*).

The dining court is shaded by black bamboo (*Phyllostachys nigra*) and underplanted with mondo grass (*Ophiopogon japonicus*) and mother ferns (*Asplenium viviparum*).

Lawn steps form a terrace that leads down to the pool.

Across the pool, the library trellis is covered with *Wisteria sinensis*.

A view of the Riviera Country Club from the pool
terrace; on the upper terrace, a lemonwood tree hedge
(*Pittosporum eugenioides*) encloses a seating area

left: The library pergola can be seen above the parterre vegetable garden, where redleaf Japanese barberry (*Berberis thunbergii 'Atropurpurea'*), mirror plant (*Coprosma repens 'Pink Splendor'*), and star jasmine (*Trachelospermum jasminoides*) grow.

above: The lower parterre garden includes vegetables, herbs, and shrubs with colored foliage.

opposite: The spa below the library terrace has a potted New Zealand peppermint tree (*Agonis flexuosa*).

Santa Monica Business Center

Santa Monica, California

A thirteen-acre business park complex in Santa Monica was built in the 1980s and, twenty years later, needed a serious overhaul. Asked to present ideas, we argued that hardscape and softscape elements could be a very effective way to transform the personality of the complex.

We worked with an energetic local team, with the goal of enhancing the property in the best way possible. It was an uplifting experience. The complex, which occupies a whole city block, consists of six separate buildings built above a subterranean, three-level parking garage and a public park. The original landscape included a perimeter of bermed lawns and overgrown fig trees that created an impenetrable fortress effect, discouraging circulation through the complex and hindering use of the exterior spaces by tenants and neighbors. The principal goal of the landscape redesign was to open the complex up and create a welcoming landscape that would improve the quality of life for the surrounding community.

We redesigned the entries to the development, opening better views into the site through selective tree relocation and pruning. We also improved exposure and visual access to the existing two-acre corner park, which was previously hidden by a berm and a heavily planted line of poplar trees. Concrete walls along the perimeter and throughout the complex were clad in a local stone, crafting the appearance of dry mortar and fitted stone. Red precast concrete pavers were replaced with blue stone pavers, creating a rich, cohesive hardscape carpet. Existing palm trees were relocated along principal pedestrian paths to create a skyline landmark, guiding visitors into the center of the development. We promoted sustainable design by introducing permeable surfaces through the elimination, when possible, of existing paving, the use of drought-tolerant Mediterranean and native plant materials, and through the placement of tree canopies to create shade. A shallow water garden with lotus and water lilies reflects the sky.

We renovated the *Pitcher Fountain* sculpture by Ron Cooper, which continually pours water into a new pool designed to be flush with the adjacent paving, resulting in a sheeting water effect. The fountain provides a focal element in the heart of the complex. Our botanical display gardens inspire and educate the community about the use of drought-tolerant plants. It is a successful integration of public and private spaces. By upgrading the landscape, we were able to help tenants, visitors, and neighbors by creating a series of garden rooms that include basketball and tennis courts, a tot lot, open lawn area, and pedestrian walks.

opposite: Aerial view of the center court entrance

136

Site plan of Santa Monica
Business Center
1 Public park
2 Ginkgo allée
3 Children's play area
4 Reflecting pond
5 Planted steps
6 Palm court
7 Aqueduct water wall
8 Plug-and-play gardens
9 Lawn steps
10 Purple plum tree grove
11 Light well for garage
12 *Jacaranda* trees

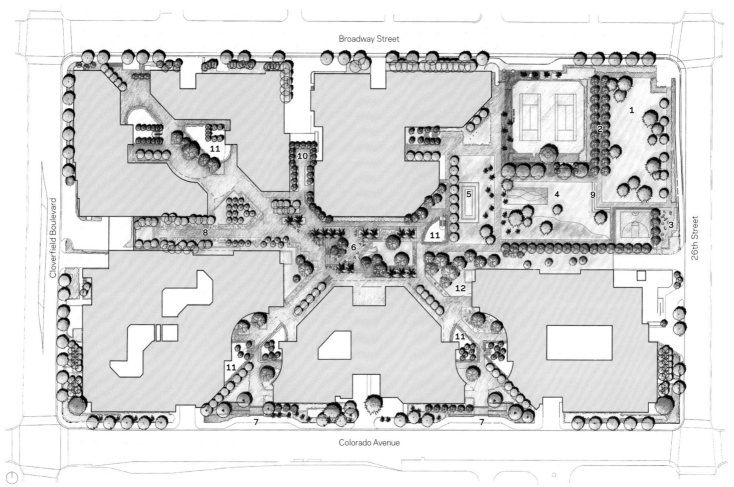

Collage showing the urban context of
Santa Monica Business Center

The center signage is mounted to an aqueduct
water wall that defines the universal ramps; lawn steps
make the transition to the public park.

138

Detail of the ellipse fountain basin

Plantings include *Festuca glauca* with islands of Japanese *Anemone* (*Anemone x hybrida*) bordered by yellow kangaroo paw (*Anigozanthus flavidos*); the walkway is lined with *Jacaranda mimosifolia* and king palms (*Archontophoenix cunninghamiana*).

Blue stone steps form a plant display of
drought-tolerant materials.

The center courtyard is the main outdoor dining space and contains Canary Island date palms (*Phoenix canariensis*) and staghorn ferns (*Platycerium bifurcatum*).

Additional seating adjacent to the center courtyard is planted with *Jacaranda mimosifolia* trees, fescues (*Festuca glauca 'Elijah Blue'*), and sweetgum trees (*Liquidambar styraciflua*).

Malibu Beach House

Malibu, California

The purpose of the landscape design was to create a colorful, sustainable garden that would tie together three oceanfront lots on Carbon Beach for which Michael Palladino, Richard Meier's West Coast partner, designed a modernist home. The big idea was to use *shakkei*, the Japanese concept of the "borrowed landscape," as a framing device; plant screen hedges block views of the Pacific Coast Highway while accentuating the nearby chaparral. The garden captures views of the adjacent hills and utilizes drought- and salt-tolerant plant materials to provide color, texture, and movement. An adjacent *arroyo*, or brook, flows toward the property, bringing rainwater. The reconstructed arroyo is a feature of the design, physically and metaphorically connecting it with the adjacent native landscape.

On this section of coastline, there is a ten- to fifteen-foot height variation between the elevation of the house and that of the beach. A wave up-rush study was required to determine the location of an underground headwall that would be located on the site. In this case, it is placed two thirds of the way between the ocean and the highway. Underground utilities, a large septic system, an underground fire suppression tank, and the headwall restricted the amount of trees that could be planted. A parking lot for four cars uses permeable paving with good percolation. The fountain and lap pool run perpendicular to the ocean, with minimal physical presence; they have an animated connection with the ocean, constantly reflecting its surface.

Originally the client expected bright green turf, which requires water. The most challenging process was to guide the client to the decision to use dry beach sand as ground cover. The sand is planted with flowing ornamental grasses that mimic the California hillsides. We wanted to demonstrate to other property owners that viable, usable, beautiful gardens can be created and maintained with minimal water.

right: Plantings include Mexican feather grass (*Nassella tenuissima*); two varieties of yellow kangaroo paw (*Anigozanthos pulcherrimus*); hybrids 'harmony,' 'bush dawn,' and 'bush gold'; and a Graham Thomas 'David Austin' rose (*Rosa 'David Austin'*) and Mexican marigold (*Tagetes lemmonii*).

opposite: To the right of the path, autumn and blue moor grasses (*Sesleria caerulea* and *Sesleria autumnalis*) combine with kangaroo paw in the distance.

Pacific Ocean

Garden

Pacific Coast Highway

Coastal Range

Site plan and illustration of the suburban context of Malibu Beach House

above: The linear water feature passes underneath an arbor with a spillway at the entry gate. Yellow flax (*Phormium 'yellow wave'*) grows under a strawberry tree (*Arbutus unedo 'Marina'*).

right: Inside the garden entry, an overhead trellis supports a Copa de Oro vine (*Solandra maxima*). The linear water feature is set flush with the walkway.

left: View of the large Indian laurel *Ficus* (*Ficus microcarpa 'Florida'*)

right: Morning light maiden grass (*Miscanthus sinensis 'Morning Light'*) and other grasses line the sandy path leading from the beach to the front entrance.

A bridge links the guesthouse with the
main deck, while an arroyo appears to flow
to the beach.

The landscape of the garden connects to
the borrowed landscape beyond.

The fern pine hedge (*Podocarpus gracilior*) screens traffic on Pacific Coast Highway.

View of the lap pool, where the bridge
connects the guest house to the main
residence.

East Fork Residence

Sun Valley, Idaho

This home in Sun Valley, Idaho, is a large property at an elevation of 7,000 feet above sea level, where there are only fifty growing days a year and the limited rainfall of the high desert. The weather is always a tricky proposition, especially in spring and fall.

The existing house was originally sited at the edge of the graded pad, placing too much emphasis on the structure. Perched on a graded prow of land, it made an inflated architectural statement, standing out amidst the vast expanse of arid high desert. The idea was to soften the prow effect by connecting the house with the landscape. We reduced the visual prominence of the house in a twofold manner. To emulate the indigenous foliage, we paid close attention to the survey and grading reports and to subtle indentations in the folds of the mountains, as they descend to the valley floor. In the folds of the surrounding mountains, through which water collects and is carried below, we planted clusters of native aspen and douglas fir trees, as well as red twig dogwood and yellow willow. As one approaches the house, these trees and bushes create a sequence of views in which the house is veiled and revealed.

In the middle of the second-floor courtyard, we emptied a swimming pool and filled it with earth. After placing dozens of huge stone planks (called "brown dog"), the courtyard floor was planted with aspen trees, *Lobelia nummularia*, and

hostas—luxuriant foliage that can survive within the protected environment. In summer, a stone, canoe-shaped vessel with bubbler jets brings the night sky down to the interior garden.

In the back are terraces with rows of crabapple trees. Along the driveway, maple trees were placed to encourage pleaching, the art of training trees into a raised hedge, like the formal rows of hornbeam trees around the Palais-Royal in Paris. The deciduous trees are planted in lines, with their branches woven together to form a flat plane above ground level.

Landscape terraces encompass the building and tie it down to the site. The series of stacked stone walls anchor the house to the earth and screen the house from the garages. They mitigate the height of the house and also provide outdoor terraces that can be used for viewing and entertaining. Planting clusters of evergreen Swedish aspens and douglas fir trees, and with the addition of the stone walls, the house was integrated with the surrounding landscape.

right: Native maple trees were planted along the driveway leading up to the house.

opposite: On the east side of the house, a series of terraces is planted with crab apple trees of different cultivars.

Site plan of East Fork Residence
1 Entrance gate
2 Douglas fir trees
3 Aspen trees
4 Red twig dogwood and yellow willows

5 Driveway through maple tree allée
6 Garages
7 Formal lawn and sculpture garden
8 Courtyard
9 Kitchen terrace

10 East crabapple terraces
11 North crabapple terraces
12 Hyndman Creek
13 Pool house and gardens

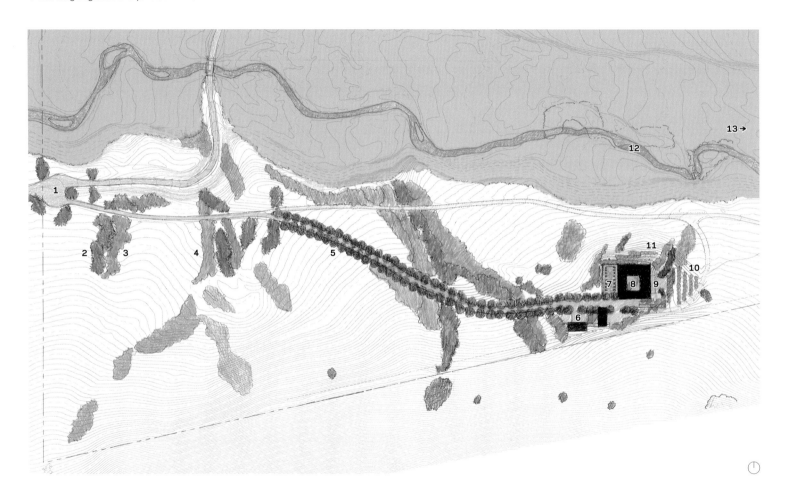

above: The house is viewed through
several veils of native douglas firs
(*Pseudotsuga menziesii*) and aspen trees
(*Populus tremuloides*) along with red twig
dogwood (*Cornus sericea*) and yellow
willow (*Salix lutea*).

right: Native high-desert foliage
blends with the stacked stone of the
avalanche wall.

Detail of the kitchen terrace interplanted
with aspen trees (*Populus tremuloides*) and
mugo pines (*Pinus mugo*).

The largest stone plank was carved like a
canoe to form a water basin.

Large planks of stone (called "brown dog") were set on the second-floor courtyard. Ground cover materials include moneywort (*Lysimachia Nummularia 'Aurea'*) and burgundy glow (*Ajuga reptans 'Burgundy Glow'*). Aspen trees (*Populus tremuloides*) were planted to extend the nearby landscape.

above: At the entrance to the mudroom, between two avalanche walls, stairs rise up to the kitchen terrace.

left: Hedges of *Spirea* magic carpet (*Spirea x bumalda 'Magic Carpet'*) and low walls flank the entrance to the front garden.

opposite: Two red granite benches by sculptor Scott Burton are placed at either end of a formal green lawn framed by Swedish aspens (*Populus tremula erecta*).

Happy Canyon Residence

Santa Ynez Valley, California

A few years after the completion of this home in Santa Ynez, I was asked to revitalize its already well-established landscape. When I visited the site, I realized that we needed to link all of the different areas around the house and make them part of a greater whole.

We sought to create an arboreal mass of trees surrounding the house to interface with the native landscape of chaparral and oak grassland. We settled on planting 250 olive trees. As a result, the first vision of the house, as one proceeds along the driveway, is through a gray-colored, foliaged olive grove. At first the deer would eat the trees; that problem was solved by a single, electric wire fence that trained the deer to not come to that part of the property.

While the lawn around the swimming pool looked good and was used, the front lawn had become an irregular patch of green; it was not useful and therefore eliminated. One problem was that the soil was composed of heavy clay, with poor percolation. We used gypsum to energize the soil and promote the growth of rhizomes. At the same time, we grouped together masses of plants at the entryway, including three types of lavender and *Teucrium*. Where one approaches the house through the pergola-covered walkway, we introduced groups of Mediterranean flowering shrubs to give the entrance new life. Throughout, we planted similar types of plants together to give an even-handed consistency to the landscape.

One of the most enjoyable parts of the project was developing a new pond. As a housewarming present, a neighbor proposed to build a pond for both families to use as fire flow, and to provide a place to ride horses and swim. An acre-and-a-half pond was created within the natural folds of the native landscape, at a meeting place for drainage swales, to minimize the amount of grading, or cut and fill. To filter the water, the pond is planted with self-sustaining aquatic plants. The pond had to be fenced in; the goal was to make the fence unobtrusive so that it disappeared within the surrounding landscape. There are planted steps leading down to the body of the pond and to a dock. The surrounding area is planted in Mediterranean materials that can withstand the heat, cold, and wind.

right: The entry drive through olive groves

opposite: Overview of the front entry with the Santa Ynez Valley below.

Site plan of Happy Canyon Residence
1 New pond
2 Entrance drive
3 Olive groves
4 Main house

bottom: Plantings around the pond include sycamores (*Platanus racemosa*) and sages (*Salvia*) integrated with the native landscape.

Mixed oaks and sycamores with *Salvias*
and Mediterranean drought-tolerant
materials form the slope of the pond area

The dock as diving platform

The Santa Ynez Mountains in the background, rolling oak grasslands, and pond plantings form a series of layers. Egyptian blue lilies (*Nymphaea*) planted on underwater shelves help to filter the water.

The yellow color of the Mexican feather grass (*Nassella tenuissima*) emulates the hues of surrounding grasslands.

Peppers (*Schinus mole*) and olives (*Olea europa*) frame the entry walk.

Precast concrete stepping stones lead
to the pergola.

right: View over the field of lavender to an adjacent hill planted with *Agave*.

opposite: Beside four different kinds of lavender, a rose-covered pergola leads to the front door.

São Paulo Esplanade

São Paulo, Brazil

We were asked by a developer to work with Aflalo & Gasperini Arquitetos in Sao Paulo to unify and personalize four new office towers situated on the Pinheiros River. We wanted the gardens to have a strong experiential presence and to hold their own. The tall, muscular office towers are handsome, dashing buildings with translucent skins, leaning into the Garden of Eden, a sunken parklike environment we created as the heart of the complex. The buildings are integrated with the surrounding urban environment by being a visible oasis for neighboring shopping centers and housing. The private garden areas that are part of Esplanade will be open for controlled but vital public access.

Our idea was to plant two layers of arboreal mass. The first layer is an overhead canopy of native *Cesalpina* trees that meanders from the river-lined side of the site to the entrance plaza. This brushstroke of native Brazilian trees will turn a golden yellow color when flush with flowers in the spring. The scale of these trees visually links the entire site together and recalls the towering trees of the rainforest and nearby jungles. The second layer of arboreal mass is a small pedestrian-scaled tree canopy, placed on the same grid as the buildings to create filtered shade and to lower the ground plane temperature. The entrance plaza is seen as a large, filtering river delta that allows visitors to meander through lushly planted gardens as they move from the city to the inner plaza spaces. Plant materials native to Brazil were used to provide color,

texture, and movement. The grid structure of the lower trees is superimposed beneath the overhead canopy of river trees within the space.

The main plaza was designed to allow access to the middle of the site by cars, over three levels of parking. Within the center of the complex we created a sunken garden surrounded by earthen berms. The berms were planted with tall grasses and shrubs to form an intensified landscape amidst the automobile traffic. Each tower entrance establishes an entry point to this Garden of Eden. Pedestrians descend slowly through circuitous paths of gravel to reach this inner garden.

A series of outdoor rooms surround the Garden of Eden; they were created using sliding bars of plant materials, amorphous masses of ornamental grasses and shrubs, and pathways made of crushed rock. The plaza gardens contrast orthogonal bars of plant materials, which align with the architecture, with free-form fields of plant materials, recalling the painterly gardens of the Brazilian architect Roberto Burle Marx. In one garden, a large wind funnel is designed to act as a chimney that draws warm air off the plaza and replaces it with cooler air from the adjacent river. This structure creates a visually arresting object, seen from cars rushing by on the freeway. In another garden, a semiprivate outdoor space for corporate events uses a series of water jets arranged to create a thirteen-foot (four-meter) tall water curtain.

opposite: Pedestrian-scaled princess flower trees (*Tibouchina urvilleana*) extend the spatial order of the buildings and surrounding landscape.

bottom: The section diagram of the site shows the pedestrian-scaled trees with the taller Pau-Brasil trees.

top right: View of Esplanade in the foreground, adjacent to the Pinheiros River

bottom right: Aerial view of the Garden of Eden built over four stories of parking; phase two will include two additional towers.

An earthen ramp on the scale of the adjacent freeway pays homage to the artist Robert Smithson. As one ascends the ramp and spirals around, there is a long view down the Pinheiros River toward the distant mountains. Within the spiral, there is a quiet, intimate space for employees. In the last garden court we capitalized on the windy vantage point adjacent to the river by using LED lights suspended on long, carbon fiber poles that sway in the wind. At night, as one drives past the site, these digital grasses create an ever-changing visual display. The landscape incorporates the earth ramp, digital lights, water jets, a wind funnel, and the sky mirrored in the reflecting pond to produce an environment that welcomes and engages visitors.

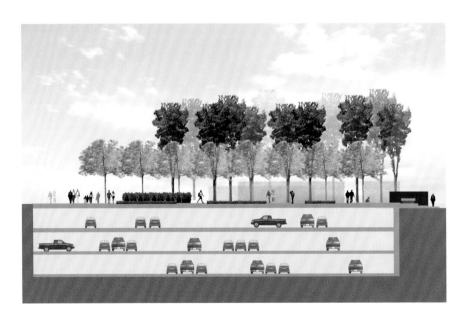

Site plan of São Paulo Esplanade
1 Lobbies
2 Pedestrian-scaled grid trees
3 High canopy river trees
4 Entrance plaza stair
5 Water garden
6 Driveway
7 Access to subterranean garage
8 Garden of Eden
9 Pedestrian path
10 Seating area
11 Spiral ramp
12 Children's play area
13 Fiber-optic light grove
14 Pinheiros River

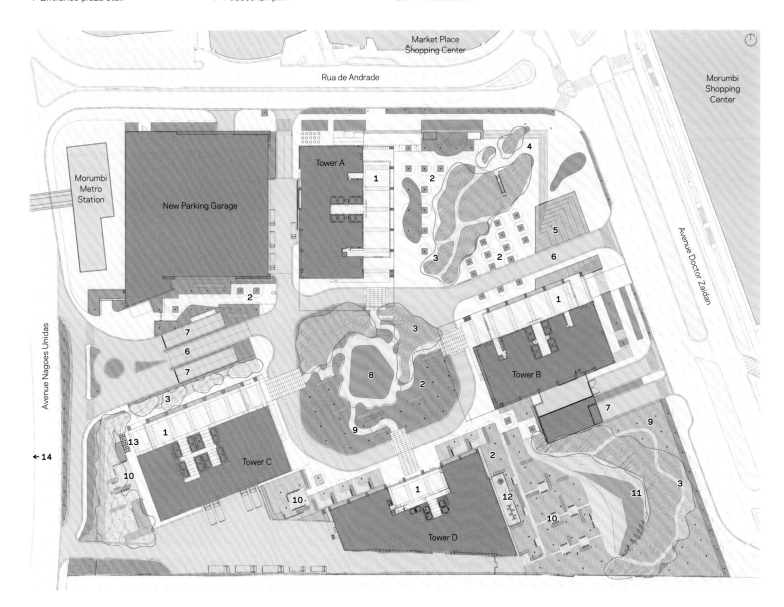

right: The entrance drive is on the right
with the stepped water feature to the left.

opposite: The granite-lined water feature
is stepped to align with the pedestrian
stair; it looks elegant even when there is
no water.

left: A custom-built, curving bench in the Garden of Eden separates the grassy berms from the central lawn.

above: Three kinds of plants form the edge of the pathway: bromeliads (*Alcantarea imperialis*), *Ctenanthe burle-marxii*, and succulents (*Tradescantia spathacea*).

opposite: Many office workers arrive by public transportation and are greeted by the plaza's parklike entrances.

opposite left: Pau-Brasil trees (*Caesalpinia echinata*) lead visitors into the site.

opposite right: Berms on each side of the path provide additional soil volume for the trees, as well as a sense of enclosure within the large space. The pavers, from a local quarry, are planted with *Paspalum* grass.

above: The rectangular geometry of the building contrasts with the sweeping Pau-Brasil trees.

right: The meandering path under the trees

left: Grassy berms in the Garden of Eden separate pedestrians from the vehicles.

above: A curving bench in the garden

opposite: A calm refuge was created in the Garden of Eden at the center of the complex by lowering the elevation and planting tall trees; their high canopies and seasonal color metaphorically bring the river into the site.

Acknowledgments

Numerous people have contributed their talents and ideas to create this book. None of the projects could have been realized without the imagination and hard work of the staff of Pamela Burton & Company, who are listed in the Staff List. For their help with the book, I would especially like to mention Robin Carmichael and Megan McAllister, who have been involved with the project from the very beginning. I am very fortunate to have the unfailing support of my colleagues Steven Billings, Stephanie Psomas, and Andrea Zurik-Klein. I extend particular gratitude to friends who have provided encouragement and guidance over many years, including John Baldessari, Bruce and Marie Botnick, Linda Brown, Michael Crichton, Nancy Englander, Gil Friesen, Suzi and Steve Gilbert, Andy Gruber, Chuck and Judy Kanner, James Manifold, Robyn Moore, Peter Morton, Matt Nye, Rob Speyer, Jane and Bill Wells, and Jann Wenner. I am grateful to Michael Webb for introducing us to Clare Jacobson at Princeton Architectural Press. Our editor Laurie Manfra has been a delight to work with, patient, inspired, and open to our suggestions. Paul Wagner's design of the book is insightful and elegant. Arla and David Manson, Jacqui Feather, and Elyn Zimmerman were invaluable in helping to structure and edit the Introduction. Special appreciation to Tassajara Zen Center in Carmel Valley, California for providing a centered environment while my husband Richard Hertz and I worked on the captions for the photographs. I would like to express my thanks to Richard for his ongoing enthusiasm as well as insightful contributions to the text. Without his devotion, this book could not have been written. Finally, I thank my children Julia and Nicholas for their love and understanding of my dedication to landscape architecture.

Project Credits

Bonhill Residence (PP. 22–35)
Location: Brentwood, California
Client name: Gil Friesen
Project size: 1.5 acres
Years: 1985–2010
Landscape architectural design team: Pamela Burton
Architect: Michael Palladino, principal, Richard Meier & Partners Architects, LLP
Landscape contractor: Ranselaar Landscaping; Royal Landscape, Inc.; NatureScape, Inc.
General contractor: Araya Construction; RJC Builders, Inc.

Colton Avenue Streetscape, University of Redlands
(PP. 36–41)
Location: Redlands, California
Client name: University of Redlands
Project size: 0.5 mile of median and parkways
Year: 1997
Landscape architectural design team: Pamela Burton, Mary Sager-McFadden
Architect: Meyer and Allen Associates, Inc.
Landscape contractor: Riverside Landscape
General contractor: Tilden Construction
Award: American Society of Landscape Architects, Southern California Chapter, Merit Award, 1997

Cantitoe Farm (PP. 42–51)
Location: Bedford, New York
Project size: 68 acres
Year: 1999
Landscape architectural design team: Pamela Burton, Prakash Pinto
Architect: Kanner Architects
Landscape contractor: Rosedale Nurseries, Inc.
General contractor: Fort Hill General Contractors

Ashley Ridge Residence
(PP. 52–61)
Location: Hidden Hills, California
Client name: Leslie and Cliff Gilbert-Lurie
Project size: 1 acre
Year: 2007
Landscape architectural design team: Pamela Burton, Stephen Billings, Andrea Zurick-Klein, Nancy B. Greene
Architect: Lise Claiborne Matthews
Landscape contractor: Royal Landscape, Inc.
General contractor: Derry Naylor (Naylor Construction Services Group)

Calabasas Civic Center
(PP. 62–67)
Location: Calabasas, California
Client name: City of Calabasas
Project size: 2 acres
Year: 2008
Landscape architectural design team: Pamela Burton, Andrea Zurik-Klein, Tom Hessel
Design architect: Robert A.M. Stern Architects, LLP

Executive architect: Harley Ellis Devereaux
Landscape contractor: Advanced Landscape 2000
General contractor: Bernards

Palm Canyon Residence
(PP. 70–77)
Location: Malibu, California
Project size: 5 acres
Year: 1996
Landscape architectural design team: Pamela Burton, Melinda Wood, Sasha Tarnopolsky, Angie Coyier
Architect: Steve Giannetti
Landscape contractor: James H. Cowan & Associates. Inc.
General contractor: Ramage Construction, Inc.

School of the Arts Plaza, University of California, Irvine (PP. 78–85)
Location: Irvine, California
Client name: School of the Arts, UCI
Project size: 2 acres
Year: 2005
Landscape architectural design team: Pamela Burton, Connie Yu, Stephanie Psomas, Angie Coyier, Jennifer Feaster, Jeremy Klemic, David Fletcher, Maria Cruz, Tom Hessel
Artist: Maya Lin
Consultants: Scaliter Irrigation Engineering, Saiful/Bouquet Structural Engineering, Nikolakopulos & Associates Electrical Engineering, Norris-Repke Civil Engineering
Landscape contractor: Flintridge Landscape

General contractor: PCL Constructors, Inc.
Fountain construction: Hobbs Architectural Fountains
Award: The Architecture Foundation of Orange County Award, 2006

Scenario Lane Residence
(PP. 86–93)
Location: Bel Air, California
Client name: Breck & Georgia Eisner
Project size: 1.5 acres
Year: 2008
Landscape architectural design team: Pamela Burton, Stephen Billings, Tom Hessel
Architect: Michael Palladino, principal, Richard Meier & Partners Architects, LLP
Landscape contractor: James H. Cowan & Associates, Inc.
General contractor: Hilgendorf Corporation

Santa Monica Public Library
(PP. 94–101)
Location: Santa Monica, California
Client name: City of Santa Monica
Project size: 2 acres
Year: 2005
Landscape architectural design team: Pamela Burton, Stephanie Psomas, Angie Coyier
Architect: Moore Ruble Yudell Architects & Planners
Landscape contractor: Reliable Landscape
General contractor: Morley Builders
Awards: American Society of Lanscape Architects, Southern California Chapter, Honor Award,

2007; California Construction Best of 2006 Merit Award; Precast Institute Design Award, Best Public/Institutional Building, 2006; Los Angeles Architectural Award, sustainable category, 2006; Calibre Award for Environmental Leadership, 2006

Red Tail Ranch (PP. 102–111)
Location: Santa Ynez, California
Client name: Jane and William Wells
Project size: 15 acres
Year: 2007
Landscape architectural design team: Pamela Burton, Stephen Billings, Nancy B. Greene
Architect: Frederick Fisher and Partners
Landscape contractor: Paysage Landscape
General contractor: Coastal Builders, Inc.

Santa Fe Industrial Complex
(PP. 112–119)
Location: Santa Fe Springs, California
Project size: 40 acres
Year: 2006
Landscape architectural design team: Pamela Burton, Stephanie Psomas, Caroline Smuckler, Matson Walter, Anna Kelly Saavedra
Architect: Steven Ehrlich Architects
Landscape contractor: Bemus Landscape, Inc.
General contractor: Pepper Construction
Award: American Society of Landscape Architects, Southern California Chapter, Honor Award, 2007

La Mesa Residence (PP. 124–133)
Location: Santa Monica, California
Project size: 1 acre
Years: 1997–2000
Landscape architectural design team: Pamela Burton, Stephanie Psomas, Stephen Billings, Matson Walter
Architect: Rockefeller Hricak Architects
Landscape contractors: James H. Cowan & Associates, Inc., Harold Jones Landscape, Inc., Four Seasons Landscape
General contractor: Winters-Schram Associates

Santa Monica Business Center
(PP. 134–141)
Location: Santa Monica, California
Client name: Tishman Speyer
Project size: 13 acres
Year: 2004
Landscape architectural design team: Pamela Burton, Stephanie Psomas, Caroline Smuckler, Anna Kelly Saavedra, Jeremy Klemic
Architect: Gensler
Landscape contractor: ValleyCrest Landscape Companies
General contractor: Matt Construction
Award: American Society of Landscape Architects, Southern California Chapter, Quality-of-Life Merit Award, 2005

Malibu Beach House (PP. 142–151)
Location: Malibu, California
Project size: 0.5 acre
Year: 2007
Landscape architectural design team: Pamela Burton,

Andrea Zurik-Klein, Stephanie Psomas, Stephen Billings
Architect: Michael Palladino, principal, Richard Meier & Partners Architects, LLP
Landscape contractor: James H. Cowan & Associates, Inc.
General contractors: Araya Construction, Inc., Hilgendorf Corporation
Sand supplier: Gordon Sand Company
Awards: American Society of Landscape Architects, Residential Design Award of Honor, 2008; American Society of Landscape Architects, Southern California Chapter, Merit Award, 2007

East Fork Residence (PP. 152–159)
Location: Triumph, Idaho
Project size: 155.6 acres
Year: 2006
Landscape architectural design team: Pamela Burton, Connie Yu, Stephen Billings, Stephanie Psomas
Architect: Lake|Flato Architects, Brian Korte
Local architect: Michael Doty Associates
Landscape contractor: All Seasons Landscaping
General contractor: Bishop Builders Inc

Happy Canyon Ranch (PP. 160–169)
Location: Santa Ynez, California
Project size: 93 acres
Year: 2007
Landscape architectural design team: Pamela Burton, Nancy B. Greene, Steve Billings

Architect: Michael Palladino, principal, Richard Meier & Partners Architects, LLP
Landscape contractor: Paysage Landscape
General contractor: Coastal Builders, Inc.

São Paulo Esplanade (PP. 170–181)
Location: Sao Paulo, Brazil
Client name: Tishman Speyer/ Autonomy Investimentos
Project size: 23 acres
Year: Phase I 2009, Phase II under construction
Landscape architectural design team: Pamela Burton, Stephanie Psomas, Stephen Billings, Robin Carmichael
Architect: Aflalo & Gasperini Arquitetos
Landscape contractor: Sergio Santana Associates
General contractor: Metodo Engenharia S.A.

Chronology

1975
Jencks Residence, Santa Monica Canyon, California (Moore Ruble Yudell, Architects & Planners)
Kahn-Albuquerque Studio & Commercial Space, Venice, California

1976
Nilsson Residence, Los Angeles, California (Eugene Kupper Architects)

1977
Singleton Residence, Los Angeles, California (Rolla Wilhite)

1983
Metro-Rail, Wilshire Alvarado Subway Station, Los Angeles, California (Gensler)

1984
Forster Residence, J. Paul Getty Trust, Santa Monica, California
Vanoff Residence, Beverly Hills, California

1986
Caper Residence, Los Angeles, California
Magnuson Residence, Westwood, California

1987 (Burton & Spitz)
Master Plan for the Northwest Campus, University of California, Los Angeles, California (Urban Innovations Group)
Ocean Park Housing, Community Corporation of Santa Monica, Santa Monica, California (Appleton & Associates, Architects)
Veteran Avenue Streetscape, University of California, Los Angeles, California

1988 (Burton & Spitz)
Ascot Reservoir, Los Angeles Department of Water and Power, Los Angeles, California
Award: City of Los Angeles Cultural Affairs Commission Award of Design Excellence for the Department of Water and Power Ascot Reservoir

1991 (Burton & Spitz)
Bioscience Library, University of California, Irvine, California (Stirling & Wilford, Design Architects IBI Group Executive Architects)
Clinical Sciences Building, University of California, San Diego, La Jolla, California (Arthur Erickson Associates)
Law School Courtyard, University of California, Los Angeles, California

1992 (Burton & Spitz)
Broadway Spring Center/Biddy Mason Park, Los Angeles Community Redevelopment Agency, Los Angeles, California (The Office of Charles and Elizabeth Lee, Architects)
Award: American Society of Landscape Architects, National Merit Award

1993 (Burton & Spitz)
W.M. Keck Joint Science Facility, The Claremont Colleges, Claremont, California (Anshen + Allen Architects)

1994
Arrowhead Regional Medical Center Replacement Project, Colton, California (BTA, Inc., Architects)
California Center for the Arts, Escondido, California (Moore Ruble Yudell, Architects & Planners)
Casey Residence, Toluca Lake, California
Corinne A. Seeds University Elementary School, University of California, Los Angeles, California (Barton Phelps, Architect)
Awards: American Institute of Architects California Council, Design Award; American Institute of Architects, Los Angeles Chapter, Design Award
Ducat Residence, Malibu, California (Rubin Ojeda Architect)
North Hollywood Pump Station, Los Angeles Department of Water and Power, North Hollywood, California (Barton Phelps, Architect)
Award: American Society of Landscape Architects, Southern California Chapter, Honor Award
Northwest Campus Housing, University of California, Los Angeles, California (Barton Myers Associates, Antoine Predock, Architect, Esherick Homsey Dodge and Davis, Design Architects, Gensler)
Ojai Valley Inn, Ojai, California (Mahan Architects)

Phoenix House, Lake View Terrace, California (Robbin Hayne Design Associates)
Scripps Quotation Walk, Scripps College, Claremont, California
Award: City of Claremont Architectural Commission, Award for Excellence in Design

1995
Bourns College of Engineering, University of California, Riverside, California (Anshen + Allen Architects)
Award: American Institute of Architects, National Honor Award
Dong-Hwa University, Hualien, Taiwan (Moore Ruble Yudell, Architects & Planners)
Harris Residence, Palm Springs, California (Marmol & Radziner, Architects)
Natividad Medical Center, Monterey County, California (BTA, Inc., Architects)
Sighvatsson Residence, Pacific Palisades, California

1996
Avery Center, California Institute of Technology, Pasadena, California (Moore Ruble Yudell, Architects & Planners)
Awards: Pasadena Beautiful Foundation Award; American School and University Design Citation
Carolwood Residence, Los Angeles, California
Millard Sheets Art Center, Scripps College, Claremont, California (Anshen + Allen Architects)
Award: City of Claremont

Architectural Commission, Award of Excellence in Design

1997

Botnick Residence, Pacific Palisades, California

Colton Avenue Streetscape and Gateways, University of Redlands, Redlands, California (Meyer & Allen Associates, Architects)
Award: American Society of Landscape Architects, Southern California Chapter, Merit Award

Hall Residence, Beverly Hills, California

Shilladay Residence, Los Angeles, California

Thue Residence, Hermosa Beach, California (Rockefeller-Hricak Architects)
Award: American Institute of Architects, Long Beach/South Bay Chapter, Merit Award

1998

City of Commerce Civic Center, City of Commerce, California (Meyer & Allen Associates, Architects)

Gibson-Wick Residence, Santa Monica, California

Gilbert Residence, Brentwood, California (Moore Ruble Yudell, Architects & Planners)

Los Angeles International Airport (LAX) Tower, Los Angeles, California (Siegel Diamond, Design Architects Holmes & Narver, Executive Architects)

Master Plan, California State University, Northridge, California
Award: American Society of Landscape Architects, Southern

California Chapter, Quality-of-Life Merit Award

Meridian Tank, Los Angeles Department of Water and Power, Highland Park, California

Smith Residence, Pacific Palisades, California

University Center, University of Redlands, Redlands, California (Meyer & Allen Associates, Architects)

1999

Founders Oak Island, Pacific Palisades, California

Kennedy-Marshall Residence, Pacific Palisades, California (Gwathmey & Siegel Architects)

Manson Residence, Los Angeles, California

2000

Imax Headquarters, Santa Monica, California (HLW Architects)

Psychiatry & Behavioral Sciences Building, Stanford University Medical Center, Stanford, California (BTA, Inc., Architects)

Riverside-Magnolia Corridor Study, Riverside, California (Moule & Polyzoides, Urban Planners)

Science Center, University of Redlands, Redlands, California (Anshen +Allen LA)

Step-Out Apartments, Los Angeles, California (Roschen Van Cleve, Architects)

2001

Brawerman Ambulatory Care, City of Hope Medical Center, Duarte, California (NBBJ Architects)

Etiwanda Avenue Extension,

California State University, Northridge, California (Wheeler & Gray Consulting Engineers)

Margarita Mendez Apartments, Los Angeles, California (Roschen Van Cleve, Architects)
Award: Association of Local Housing Finance Agencies and National Association of County Community Economic Development

Rothenberg Residence, Carpenteria, California

SanFair Bus Stop Garden & Pocket Park, West Hollywood, California (Barbara McCarren, Artist)

2002

Administration Building, California State University, Northridge, California (Hardy, Holzman, Pfeiffer Associates)

Fine Arts Seismic Replacement Facility, University of California, Riverside, California (Israel Callas Shortridge Associates and Chu + Gooding Architects, Design Architects, Fields & Devereaux, Executive Architects)
Award: American Institute of Architects, Los Angeles Chapter, Merit Award

Habitat for Humanity Planned Unit Development, Wilmington, California (Roschen Van Cleve, Architects)

Houston's Cowboy Seafood Restaurant, Newport Beach, California (Frederick Fisher & Partners, Architects)

Interdisciplinary Sciences Building, University of California, Santa

Cruz, California (Moore Ruble Yudell, Architects & Planners, and Esherick Homsey Dodge and Davis, Architects)

Lantana, Santa Monica, California (Steven Ehrlich Architects)

Manson Residence, Ojai, California

Master Plan, The Webb Schools, Claremont, California

Ninth & Columbia Campus Entry, Scripps College, Claremont, California

Science Library, University of California, Riverside, California (Shepley, Bulfinch, Richardson and Abbott, Design Architects, Ehrlich Rominger, Executive Architects)

2003

1925 Bundy, Los Angeles, California (Clive Wilkinson, Architects)

Activision, Santa Monica, California
Award: American Society of Landscape Architects, Southern California Chapter, Quality-of-Life Merit Award

Horace Mann Elementary School, San Jose, California (Moore Ruble Yudell, Architects & Planners, and BCFG Architects)

Linda Burnham, Glendale, California (Stan Allen, Architect)

Plummer Park Community Center, West Hollywood, California (Koning Eizenberg Architects)
Award: American Institute of Architects, Los Angeles Chapter, Merit Award

Smalley-Wall Residence, Beverly Hills, California

Sather-Browne, Pacific Palisades, California

Vista Pacifica, Baldwin Hills
Scenic Overlook, Baldwin Hills,
California (Safdie-Rabines,
Architects)

2004

Aivazovskoje Resort Master Plan,
Black Sea, Ukraine
Baldessari Residence, Santa Monica,
California (Godfredsen Sigal)
Encino-Tarzana Branch Library, Los
Angeles, California (Steven Ehrlich
Architects)
Fashion Institute of Design
Management, Irvine, California
(Clive Wilkinson, Architects)
Helford Clinical Research Hospital,
City of Hope Medical Center,
Duarte, California (NBBJ
Architects)
Otis College of Art & Design, Los
Angeles, California (Fredrick
Fisher & Partners)
Parc Ridge Apartments, Northridge,
California (REA, Architects)
Awards: Golden Nugget Merit
Award for Affordable Projects;
Los Angeles Business Community
Affordable Housing Award
Ruscha Residence, Malibu, California
Santa Ynez Water Quality
Improvement Project, Los Angeles
Department of Water & Power,
Pacific Palisades, California
Stanford Health Care, Stanford
University Health Services
Stanford, California (BTA, Inc.,
Architects)
Toyosu Housing, Tokyo, Japan
(Impact Design, Inc., Architects)
Yokohama Housing, Yokohama,
Japan (Impact Design, Inc.,
Architects)

2005

Brown Beach House, Malibu,
California
Engineering Building Unit 2,
University of California, Riverside,
California (RBB Architects)
Foot Cone & Belding Worldwide,
Irvine, California (Clive Wilkinson,
Architects)
Ikonobe Cho, Yokohama, Japan
(Impact Design, Inc., Architects)
Intercollegiate Athletic Building,
University of California, Santa
Barbara, California (Cannon
Design Architects)
Plant Growth Center, University of
California, Los Angeles, California
(Paul Murdoch Architects)
Award: American Institute of
Architects, Los Angeles Chapter,
NEXT LA AWARD
Minna Mitchell Garden, Jewish Home
for the Aging, Eisenberg Campus,
Reseda, California (Mulder Katkov
Architects)
Westwood Library, Los Angeles,
California (Steven Ehrlich
Architects)

2006

Bruggemeyer Library, Monterey
Park, California (Paul Murdoch
Architects)
Farmer's Market, Los Angeles,
California (Koning Eizenberg
Architects) Awards: Los Angeles
Architectural Award; Urban Land
Institute Award for Excellence
Tierra del Sol, Canoga Park,
California (Hak Sik Son and DEA
Architects)
United States Courthouse, Fresno,
California (Moore Ruble Yudell

Architects & Planners)
Award: U.S. General Services
Administration Honor Award

2007

Arroyo Grill, California State
University, Northridge, California
(Harley Ellis Devereaux Architects
and Engineers)
La Cienega Development, Los
Angeles, California (HLW
International Architects)
Madison Theater, Santa Monica
College, Santa Monica, California
(Renzo Zecchetto Architects)
Maple Drive Office, Beverly
Hills, California (Walter Meyer
Architects)
Maple Plaza, Beverly Hills, California
South Houses, California Institute of
Technology, Pasadena, California
(Pfeiffer Partners Architects)
Sweetwater Mesa, Malibu, California
Thornton Lofts, Venice, California
(Michael W. Folonis & Associates,
Architects)

2008

College of Humanities, Arts & Social
Sciences, University of California,
Riverside, California (Pei Cobb
Freed, and Leo A. Daly)
Glean Residence, Brentwood,
California
Loker Student Union, California
State University, Dominguez
Hills, California (Yazdani Studio of
Cannon Design)
Rockefeller Center Plaza, New York,
New York
Steenburgen-Danson, Ojai, California
Sanders, Santa Ynez, California
Zimmerman, Ojai, California

2009

The Century, Century City, California
(Robert A.M. Stern Architects, and
HKS, Inc.)
Clinic Addition, House Ear Institute,
Los Angeles, California (Perkins +
Will Architects)
Holy Family Chapel, Santa Monica
Mountains, California (with
Kirkpatrick Associates Architects)
K & L Gates, Pittsburgh,
Pennsylvania (Lehman Smith
Macleish Architects)
Price Center Expansion, University
of California, San Diego, La Jolla,
California (Yazdani Studio of
Cannon Design)
Rader, La Quinta, California (X-Ten
Architects)
Santa Monica UCLA Medical Center
and Orthopaedic Hospital, Santa
Monica, California (with Robert
A.M. Stern, Design Architects CO
Architects, Executive Architects)
Science Building Replacement,
California State University,
Northridge, California (Yazdani
Studio of Cannon Design)
Award: American Institute of
Architects, Los Angeles Chapter,
NEXT LA AWARD
Student Services Complex,
University of California, Riverside,
California (KMD Architects)
Teviot, Hudson Valley, New York

Selected Bibliographies

Articles and books by Pamela Burton:

"Appropriating English Archetypes." *Landscape Architecture*, June 1988, 55–59.

"Architecture in the Community Issue." *arcCA*, August 2008, 14.

"Burton's Way." *Western Interiors and Design,* May/June 2006, 47–52.

"Firestorms: Re-ordering California Landscapes." *Landscape Australia*, 1994.

Garden Design Conference, March 1994, 208–11.

"Healing and Cultivation." Coauthored by Richard Hertz. *Modulus 20,* (May 1991): 84–87.

"I Love This Plant: Sharkskin Agave." *Garden Design*, February 2007, 14.

"The Language of Scripted Spaces." Coauthored by Richard Hertz. *Landscape Review*, September 1996, 24–32.

"Modern Wonder." *Garden Design*, October 2000, 23.

"Modernism Now (and Forever!)." *Garden Design Magazine,* October 2005, 49–51.

"Something Borrowed." *Garden Design*, November/December 2008, 82.

Private Landscapes: Modernist Gardens in Southern California. Coauthored by Marie Botnick, with an introduction by Kathryn Smith. New York: Princeton Architectural Press, 2002.

Articles and books about Pamela Burton:

Amidon, Jane. *Radical Landscapes: Reinventing Outdoor Space.* New York: Thames and Hudson, 2001.

Anderton, Frances. *Moore Ruble Yudell Architects and Planners.* Shenyang, China: Liaoning Science and Technology Publishing House, 2007.

Byrd, Warren T. "2008 ASLA Awards." *Landscape Architecture*, August 2008, 114–31.

Clarke, Gerald "Demi Moore & Ashton Kutcher: A Contemporary Family Home in Beverly Hills Reveals the Couple's Private Side." *Architectural Digest*, March 2007, 172–77.

———. "Michael Crichton." *Architectural Digest*, July 2002, 102–9.

Cohen, Edie. "A River Runs Through it." *Interior Design*, July 2007, 250–57.

Colman, David. "Out in the Garden, A Reputation Blooms." *New York Times*, July 11, 2003.

Dorian, Donna. "A Classical Revival." *Garden Design*, September 2006, 52–63.

———. "Endless Summer." *Los Angeles Times Magazine*, April 2006, 31–32.

Drohojowska-Philp, Hunter. "Bungalow Baldessari." *Western Interiors & Design*, July/August 2004, 110–19.

Giovannini, Joseph. "Modernism Revisited." *Architectural Digest,* July 2003, 114–21.

Godfrey, Anne. "Commercial Photography and the Understanding of Place." *Landscape Architecture*, April 2006, 34–44

Green, Emily. "Sturdy Ancient Grace." *Los Angeles Times*, June 5, 2003.

Hawthorne, Christopher. "Multiple Personalities." *Los Angeles Times*, October 11, 2008.

———. "Park Offers Views of L.A. Development." *Los Angeles Times*, April 25, 2009.

Heeger, Susan. "Telling Stories: Pamela Burton's Gardens." *Garden Design*, May 1997, 48–57.

Keeney, Gavin. *On the Nature of Things: Contemporary American Landscape Architecture.* Basel, Switzerland: Birkhauser, 2000.

Sasken, Louis and Michael Bobrow. "Cancer Care in a Garden." *Healthcare Design*, May 2004, 62–69.

Symmes, Marilyn, ed. *Fountains: Splash and Spectacle: Water and Design from the Renaissance to the Present.* New York: Rizzoli, 1998.

Trulove, James Grayson. *25 Houses Under 2500 Square Feet.* New York: Collins Design, 2005.

———. *Pocket Gardens: Big Ideas for Small Spaces.* New York: William Morrow, 2000.

———. *The New American Garden: Innovations in Residential Landscape Architecture: 60 Case Studies.* New York: Whitney Library of Design, 1998.

Webb, Michael. "Two Beach Houses in Malibu, California, USA Richard Meier & Partners Architects." *The Plan*, December 2008, 160.

Yudell, Buzz, and John Ruble. *Moore Ruble Yudell: Making Places.* Victoria, Australia: Images Publishing Group, 2004.

Studio Profile

Pamela Burton

Stephanie Psomas

Andrea Zurik-Klein

Stephen Billings

Pamela Burton, FASLA

Pamela Burton received her bachelor of arts and master of architecture degrees from the University of California, Los Angeles (UCLA). Motivated to integrate the disciplines of art, architecture, and landscape, she founded Pamela Burton & Company shortly after graduation. The Santa Monica–based corporation offers comprehensive landscape design for civic, institutional, commercial, and residential clients.

In spring 2002, Burton coauthored with Marie Botnick *Private Landscapes: Modernist Gardens in Southern California*. The book profiles residential gardens designed by midcentury modernists Richard Neutra and Rudolph Schindler, as well as a number of their colleagues. The book was published by Princeton Architectural Press.

Burton's projects include private residences and public landscapes in California, Idaho, New York, Brazil, Japan, Korea, and Taiwan. She combines her passions for plant materials and the history of landscape architecture to create designs that evolve from a site's cultural and physical environment. Her work is informed by geography, ecology, and history. Setting up displacements within a rationally ordered grid, she introduces metaphorical themes and layerings of history to produce resonant spaces. As principal of the firm, Burton oversees conceptual design and plays a critical role in site and program analysis, design development, client presentations, and construction observation.

Burton is a Fellow of the American Society of Landscape Architects. She has taught and lectured on the significance of landscape and its relationship to art and architecture at many universities, including the UCLA School of Architecture, the University of Southern California, and the Southern California Institute of Architecture. Her explorations in landscape have led to design symposia and international speaking engagements on such topics as "Garden as Sanctuary," "Memory and Landscape," "Balance and Uncertainty," and "Poetics of the Garden."

Stephanie Psomas, ASLA

Stephanie Psomas graduated from the Otis Art Institute and from the UCLA Extension Program in Landscape Architecture. Her passion for horticulture and the wealth of plant materials that thrive in Southern California is the source of motivation for her ongoing quest for unusual trees and shrubs that can be incorporated into projects.

Psomas joined Pamela Burton & Company in 1987 when she was assigned project management duties for Broadway Spring Center–Biddy Mason Park. Her innovative approach to project organization and coordination has been evident in subsequent municipal, commercial, institutional, and residential work. These include the California Center for the Arts in Escondido, UCLA Northwest Campus Housing, Colorado Center in Santa Monica, as well as numerous projects for the Los Angeles

Department of Water and Power. Her understanding of water-use issues, material upkeep, and replacement and security concerns helps ensure the design of environments that will be sustainable and attractive for many years.

Project director for some of Pamela Burton & Company's major collaborations, she assists in quality control and lends her expertise in specification writing and budgeting analysis. As director of operations, Psomas heads the firm's development and marketing activities and oversees human resource, and office management.

Psomas is a registered landscape architect and a member of the American Society of Landscape Architects. She is also a member of the American Horticulture Society and has participated in numerous educational programs for the UCLA Extension Landscape Architecture Program.

Andrea Zurik-Klein, ASLA

Andrea Zurik-Klein received her bachelor of fine arts and bachelor of landscape architecture degrees from the Rhode Island School of Design and her master of landscape architecture degree from the Harvard University Graduate School of Design. She has worked with a number of design firms in the United States and Asia, including Edward Durell Stone Jr. & Associates, Universal Studios Creative, the Boston Redevelopment Authority, and Carol R. Johnson Associates Landscape Architects.

Zurik-Klein has collaborated on a variety of projects in the United States and abroad. These include theme parks, resorts, mixed-use commercial developments, historic preservation, recreational facilities, and residential developments in California, New England, the British Virgin Islands, Japan, and China. She is devoted to creating sustainable environments that stimulate, heal, and enrich the quality of life. She applies this approach to her work in healthcare design, justice facilities, and large-scale residential, municipal, and institutional projects.

As senior project manager at Pamela Burton & Company, Zurik-Klein has designed and managed a variety of projects including: the Calabasas Civic Center, the Ventura County Juvenile Justice Center, the Century Luxury Condominiums in Century City, the Santa Barbara Airline Terminal Improvements Project, and the American Institute of Taiwan in Taipei.

Zurik-Klein is a registered landscape architect and a member of the American Society of Landscape Architects, the California Native Plant Society, and the Garden Conservancy.

Stephen Billings, AIA, ASLA
Born and raised in coastal South Carolina, Stephen Billings has more than ten years of experience in architecture and six years in landscape architecture. He received his bachelor of architecture degree from Syracuse University, and his masters of landscape architecture degree from the Harvard University Graduate School of Design. He worked with Paolo Soleri on the construction of a prototypical city—the Arcosanti project—in Arizona. He has also worked with Richard Meier & Partners Architects In Los Angeles and with Michael Van Valkenburgh Associates in New York City.

Billings's understanding of what it takes to design, detail, manage, and construct buildings and spaces led to his commitment to collaborate with architects and urban designers to create social spaces in the landscape. He is focused on landscape design that combines the spatial experiences of buildings with landscape strategies that incorporate ecology, water resource management, and sustainable design practices. His goal is to amplify the multilayered experiences of a particular site.

As senior project manager at Pamela Burton & Company, Billings has provided design leadership on projects throughout the United States, Mexico, and Brazil. He has designed and managed a wide range of project types, including rooftop and plaza-level renovations at Rockefeller Center, the Valley Performing Arts Center at California State University at Northridge, a large commercial project in Brazil, a hotel in Hollywood, renovations to the Museum of Tolerance in Los Angeles, primary and secondary schools, university and corporate campuses, art galleries, and residential projects throughout Southern California, Mexico City, and the Hudson River Valley.

Billings is a registered landscape architect and a member of the American Society of Landscape Architects. He is also a member of the American Institute of Architects. He teaches landscape architecture at Otis College of Art and Design. He has taught a design studio for the Career Discovery Program at the Harvard University Graduate School of Design, and has been a design critic at the Southern California Institute of Architecture and UCLA.

Staff List

Caroline Abrahamson
Isabelle Albuquerque
Cam Amos
Elizabeth Benbrooks
Robin Benezra
Tracy Benford Smith
Chanon Billington
Robin Carmichael
Claudia Carol
Jennifer Cosgrove
Angie Coyier
Dave Davies
Joe De Soussa
Rodrigo de Mendoza
Angela Denby
Derrick Eichelberger
Jennifer Feaster
David Fletcher
Steven Flood
Pablo Garcia
Tom Gibson
Nancy Greene
Linda Grove
Victoria Haviland
Tom Hessel
Veenu Jayaram
Sarah Jones
Barbara Kaplan
Ceyrena Kay
Jeremy Klemic
Clare Koslow
Marti Kyrk
Kirsten Leitner
Marissa Levin
James Lippincott
Mike Lombardi
Patrick Lynch

Andrea Magolske
Megan McAllister
Susan McCarthy
Karol Morera
Darin Morris
Doreen Morrissey
Sasha Musa
Scott Neiman
Mary Padua
Jose Parral
Prakash Pinto
David Pura
Dan Rhodes
Stephen Richards
Ashton Rosendahl
Anna Kelly Saavedra
Mary Sager McFadden
Ami Sakamoto
Josh Segal
Aaron Spell
Katherine Spitz
Michelle Sullivan
Lisa Swanson
Sasha Tarnopolsky
Nick Tessa
Matson Walter
Gary Weiss
Melinda Wood
Mao Yik
Connie Yu

Photo Credits

All plan drawings by Pamela Burton & Company Landscape Architects.

pp. 8-17: 1: Elyn Zimmerman; 2-4: Pamela Burton; 5: Dextra Frankel; 6: Near Paradise, by Astrid Preston, 1986; 7: Eugene Kupper; 8: John Baldessari Studio; 9-10: Pamela Burton

Part I
pp. 18-21: 1: Tim Street-Porter; 2-5: Pamela Burton
Bonhill Residence: all photographs by Jack Coyier.
Colton Avenue Streetscape, University of Redlands: all photographs by Steve Hug
Canitoe Farm: all photographs by Steve Kahn
Ashley Ridge Residence: all photographs by Jack Coyier
Calabasas Civic Center: all photographs by Jack Coyier

Part II
pp. 68-69: 1-4: Pamela Burton
Palm Canyon Residence: all photographs by Jack Coyier
School of the Arts Plaza, University of California, Irvine: all photographs by Bruce Botnick
Scenario Lane Residence: all photographs by Jack Coyier
Santa Monica Public Library: p. 94: photograph by Edward Linden; p. 97: photograph by Kenneth Naverson; p. 98 above right and p. 100 above: photographs by

Bruce Botnick; all other photographs by Jack Coyier
Red Tail Ranch: all photographs by Bruce Botnick
Santa Fe Industrial Complex: pp. 116 and 117 above right: Julia Schmidt; pp. 117 below and 119: Tom Bonner

Part III
pp. 120-123: 1-2: Anne Godfried; 3-7: Pamela Burton; 8-9: Tim Street-Porter; 10: Pamela Burton
La Mesa Residence: all photographs by Jack Coyier
Santa Monica Business Park: pp. 135, 137 bottom, 138 left and bottom, 139, 140, and 141: photographs by Jack Coyier; all other photographs by Pamela Burton
Malibu Beach House: p. 151: photograph by Pamela Burton; all other photographs by Bruce Botnick
East Fork Residence: all photographs by Steve Kahn
Happy Canyon Ranch: all photographs by Jack Coyier
São Paulo Esplanade: all photographs by Tuca Reines